Meditation and Qigong Mastery
by Ricardo B Serrano, R.Ac.

A Guide for Healing, Inner Happiness and Spiritual Awakening
by Activating and Developing Your Lightbody

"Where awareness (or attention) goes, energy flows
Where energy flows, awareness follows."

Copyright © Holisticwebs.com

All rights reserved. Reproduction of this work,
in whole or in part, without the written permission
of the author is strictly prohibited.

This book is for educational and reference purposes only.
Its contents are not intended as, nor are they a substitute for,
personal one-on-one diagnosis or treatment by, or consultation with,
a licensed health care practitioner.

Meditation and Qigong Mastery by Ricardo B Serrano (1950 –)
ISBN – 978-0-9877819-0-1

First published August 27, 2011
© Holisticwebs.com
601, 110 West 4th Street
North Vancouver, BC V7M3H3
Canada

Dedications

This book is dedicated to my parents, grandparents, siblings, wife, children, grandchildren and to the dedicated practitioners of yoga, meditation and Qigong of every tradition everywhere.

"The ultimate Consciousness is always present everywhere. It is beyond space and time, with not before or after. It is undeniable and obvious. So what can be said about it?"
- Abhinavagupta

"Oh Devi, You are existing in each and every form, in each and every step, in each and every movement of this world." - Abhinavagupta

"Absolute consciousness is manifest here in every circumstance of daily life because it is everywhere full and perfect. Consciousness is said to be the cause of all things because it is everywhere emergent as each manifest entity." — Abhinavagupta

"Tell me, what is the absolute nature of reality which allows no room for doubt? Listen carefully! Stop holding on to this or that, inhabit your true absolute nature, and peacefully enjoy the essence of what it is to be alive! Drama is like a dream, it is not real, but it is really felt." – Abhinavagupta

"Pure, Undivided Consciousness is the Highest Reality of the universe. It is the foundation of all things. It is the life-force of the universe through which the universe lives and breathes. That alone am I." - Shri Abhinavagupta

"Other achievements are in vain if one has missed the supreme reality, the Self. But once one has attained this reality there is nothing left that one could desire." - Abhinavagupta

"Moksa or liberation is nothing else but the awareness of one's true nature."
- Abhinavagupta, Tantra I, p. 192, See Quotations from Siddha tradition, page 54

Table of Contents

- Dedications . . . 3
- Introduction . . . 6
- Hunab Ku, The Mayan Solar God: The Source of Enlightenment for the Mayans . . . 7
- Galactic Center Alignment . . . 9
- Acharya Ricardo's Notes . . . 12
- Rising Earth Kundalini (Serpent of Light) & Kundalini Awakening . . . 13
- Serpent of Light Beyond 2012 . . . 18
- Kundalini Shakti (Sri Devi) . . . 21
- Hologram of Love Merkaba . . . 22
- Quotations on the Flower of Life Hologram of Love . . . 26
- The All-knowing, All-seeing divine eye of God with Mantras . . . 27
- The Heart of Prajna Paramita Sutra . . . 29
- Kundalini Awakening in the Mayan Pyramids . . . 31
- A Magical Mystery Tour of Teotihuacan . . . 33
- Maitreya (Shiva) Shen Gong . . . 34
- The Use of Qigong to Develop Your Energy Bubble . . . 37
- Who Am I? . . . 39
- Quotations on the Inner Way . . . 40
- Quotations on Inner Mastery . . . 44
- Quotations from the Power of Now & A New Earth . . . 49
- Quotations from the Power of Now . . . 51
- Quotations from A New Earth . . . 53
- Quotations from the Ancient Siddha Lineage Tradition . . . 54
- Vagus Nerve Qi-healing . . . 58
- Reasons to Address Your Stress . . . 59
- Qi-healing COVID-19 naturally . . . 61
- The Three Treasures Jing, Qi and Shen . . . 62
- How to Achieve Stillness . . . 67

- Cultivating Qi in the Hara & Its Energetic Pathways . . . 68
- Hara & Energetic Pathways Illustration . . . 71 Wing Chun & Qigong . . . 72
- Cultivating Qi in the Hara & Its Energetic Pathways (2) . . . 73
- Tancheon or Lower Dantian Breathing . . 76 Wing Chun Rules of Conduct . . 78
- The Three Dantians . . . 79 Keys and Maxims of Wing Chun . . . 81
- Chinese Medical Qigong Therapy . . . 82 Wing Chun Training Proverbs . . . 83
- Chinese Tonic Herbs to Cultivate Jing, Qi and Shen . . . 84
- Intranasal Light Therapy . . . 94
- Ricardo B Serrano's Story . . . 95
- The Five Agreements . . . 100
- Buddha Quotations . . . 101
- Can You Hear the Mountain Stream? . . . 106
- Good and Bad . . . 107
- Is That So? . . . 108
- This, too, will pass . . . 109
- Conclusion . . . 110
- References & Recommended Books . . . 115
- Glossary of Terms . . . 116
- Flower of Life . . . 118
- Sri Yantra . . . 119
- Quotations on the mantra OM . . . 120
- Mantra of Compassion OM MANI PADME HUM . . . 122
- Vajra Guru Mantra OM AH HUM VAJRA GURU PADMA SIDDHI HUM . . . 125
- What Buddha Nature Is & Illustration . . . 129
- Guru Yoga: Merging with the Wisdom Mind of the Master . . . 130
- Guru Yoga: According to the Preliminary Practice of Longchen Nyingthig 134
- Merkaba Energy Power Ball of Light & Holographic Sound Healing . . . 136
- Why the health care system is broken . . 138 About Ricardo B Serrano . . 139

DISCLAIMER: Ricardo will not be held liable for any adverse effects arising from the meditation practices. The physical and psychological conditions of each person vary. If adverse effects are experienced, stop the practice of the meditations immediately.

Introduction

The uniqueness and main emphasis of this book "Meditation and Qigong Mastery" that is lacking in other meditation and Qigong books is in activating and developing your energy bubble, also called merkaba (lightbody), Wei Qi or EMF (electromagnetic field) through the use of breathing, Omkabah Lightbody Activation meditation and Maitreya (Shiva) Shen Gong that, I believe, is the missing ancient divine key for healing, inner happiness and spiritual awakening. This book is a supplementary reading material to the other six books and videos on Kundalini Awakening, Omkabah Lightbody Activation and Maitreya (Shiva) Shen Gong published by Ricardo B Serrano, R.Ac.

The mission of this book is Self-Realization, inner happiness and healing through the use of Meditation, herbs, Qi-healing by intranasal light therapy and Qigong as stated below:

The mission of Meditation and Qigong Mastery (Inner Way) facilitated by Ricardo B Serrano, R.Ac. in Vancouver, B.C. is to assist clients to achieve healing, inner happiness and spiritual awakening through the integration of breathing with postures, meditation, herbs, Qigong, and light therapy to cultivate the three treasures Jing, Qi, and Shen together with Toltec wisdom, Sri Vidya and Tantric spiritual teachings.

In my over 30 years of study and practice, as an Oriental medicine practitioner, in meditation and Qigong from teachers of various traditions ~ non-sectarian Kashmir Shaivism, Buddhism, Shamanism, Taoism, Sacred Geometry, Tantrism, etc, ~ it all boils down to one thing, i.e. how to manage day-to-day stress to maintain holistic health and well-being by being spiritually awakened ~ through breathing, meditation, herbs, Qigong, and light therapy that mainly cultivate the three treasures Jing, Qi and Shen.

I founded Vancouver Qigong Mastery (Inner Way) to share the ancient breathing, meditation and Qigong practices because I have sincerely been spiritually awakened, and have benefited from their daily practice in managing stress which is the main cause of disease.

If you are interested to learn the breathing, meditation and Qigong practices of Vancouver Qigong Mastery individually or in a group setting, please email me at vancouver@qigongmastery.ca or call 604-987-1797 for appointment. Thank you for your interest!

Ricardo B Serrano, R.Ac
http://www.qigongmastery.ca

With much thanks and acknowledgements to my following teachers don Miguel Ruiz, Alton Kamadon, Drunvalo Melchizedek, Eckhart Tolle, Karlfried Graf Durckheim, Baba Muktananda, Swami Laksmanjoo, Ron Teeguarden, Master Choa Kok Sui, Kiiko Matsumoto, Stephen Birch, Hyunmoon Kim, Patricia Cardona, Jerry Allan Johnson, Lama Tantrapa, Li Jun Feng, Michael Winn, Richard Mooney, Ou Wen Wei, and Hunbatz Men, Sifu Samuel Kwok, Dr. Lew Lim, ND with Sri Vidya teacher Raja Choudhury for the inclusion of their compiled articles for the educational benefit of my students and clients.

Hunab Ku, the Mayan Solar God
The Source of Enlightenment for the Mayans

Quotations on the Mayan Solar God

"By the year 2001 will be in more of the year than out. By 2012 earth's entire orbit will be in the photon belt. The most intense part of the transition will be when our Sun moves fully into the Photon Belt in late 1998 or early 1999 - the apex of the predicted earth changes. The action of the photon belt, will also have significant effect on the pineal gland. That's why everyone's psychic energy is starting to ramp up. Barbara HC theorizes that the photon action will have a lot to do with unlocking and decoding our DNA for the next leap in evolution. Understanding these cycles is crucial to the awakening process we are all experiencing and will help reduce the physical, mental and emotional shock of this transition." - Barbara Hand Clow, Age of Light

"Through Solar Initiation they will be able to see the luminosity of the Great Spirit...through Solar Initiation, the sleeping body of humankind can be awakened..."Hunab K'u (Creator) will flash like lightening that will pierce through the shadows that envelop the human race. Let us prepare to receive the light of knowledge" (paraphrased Mayan prophesy)."

"We create our Reality. For whatever reason or purpose, the mass consciousness of humanity is embracing linear time and creating a very limited reality. As each of us shifts out of the mass consciousness, it helps to change the whole. Love and Honor your Mother Earth. Receive the Galactic Synchronization Beam from the Sun. Sing the song of your Soul. Listen to your Heart."

"There is only one Supreme God who is Omnipresent. The presence of God in the planet Earth is called the Planetary God or the Planetary Parabrahman. The planetary God is also called Planetary Logos since life on the planet Earth, physical and non-physical, is sustained through the constant use of the Sound or the Word. Logos is a Greek term for the Word or Logos. The Planetary Logos is a part of the Supreme God and is spiritually one with the Supreme God. Therefore, there is only One God. The presence of the Supreme God, in the sun and in the solar system, is called the Solar God. In the Indian tradition, the Solar Parabrahman is called Lord Surya or Lord Savitur. In the Egyptian tradition, Amen Ra. Ra means Sun. Amen Ra means the Solar God." -- Master Choa Kok Sui from Sutra 36, 37 and 38 of *The Existence of God is Self-evident*.

Galactic Center Alignment

There are many theories from many authors and researchers regarding the coming December 21, 2012. Mayans intended for 2012 not to be viewed as a final ending but rather a time of spiritual transformation and renewal. This rare galactic center alignment with our sun which occurs every 26,000 years is like an opening conduit bringing more energy into our energy vibrational field. Personally, there will be a positive turning event for the vibrational field shift of Mother Earth. However, the energy field of each individual has to be prepared for the smooth transition of mother earth's vibrational change. All those who are able to change with the vibrational shift will move towards the center of the energy vibrational field that is quiet and peaceful. All those who are not able to change and is heavy and dense will move to the edge of the energy field and experience the intensity of the energy at the outside of the energy vibrational field.

Most people would rather be in the center of the energy vibrational field that surrounds our body where it is quiet, peaceful and calm. In order to be in the center of the energy bubble, it is necessary to change our personal energy field (energy bubble). The question is how do we change our own energy bubbles to go along with the changes that are occuring in the energy vibrational fields (Light Grid) of Mother Earth?

"The Omkabah Heart Lightbody Activation and/or Maitreya Shen Gong practice will assist your energy field to make the vibrational shift in 2012 and beyond to synchronize with the vibrational shift of Mother Earth's light grid."
~ Ricardo B Serrano

"Once you have remembered and activated your lightbody, you can never lose connection to it and to the Divine." ~ Master Thoth

Quotations from Patricia Cardona

According to Patricia Cardona, "One way to teach our own bodies energy field to vibrate along with that of mother earth is to work with the sacred energy sites on the planet. These sacred sites hold the keys to learning how to change our energy vibration fields. There are sacred sites all over Mother Earth. Some of them are well known. We know they were used in the distant past, because the peoples of those times left monuments at these sites that still exist today. The pyramids of Egypt, the Sphinx, the Mayan Pyramids, Stonehenge, Mesa Verde, etc., are just a few of the well-known sacred sites. These sites hold knowledge, energy vibration and information that is still accessible today.

When Mystery School members do sacred ceremony at these sites at specific times of the year it opens their nervous systems to previously unavailable information. Just as the frequencies and intensities of solar energy affect and change the leaves on trees at specific times of the year, solar frequencies at the vernal and autumnal equinox and summer and winter solstice affect and change our nervous systems, allowing our energy vibrational fields to match those of the planet. These changes lead to greater connection with our universe, world and people on the planet, which are also vibrationally changing in this time of change. This greater connection to Cosmic Consciousness leads to greater knowing, which is a form of Intuition: knowing from feeling.

These changes in our nervous systems may initially be profound or subtle, but are always manifest. They manifest in unique ways in each individual depending on which physical and/or psychological blocks are present. As the blocks clear over time, a relationship with the greater consciousness becomes manifest for the individual. The individual begins to know beyond their current time frame or belief system. They come into Cosmic Consciousness.

Continue...

These sacred sites hold information built into them in many ways. Buildings, temples and pyramids at these sites were constructed in certain patterns using sacred geometry to help activate the higher nervous system. Drawings and glyphs on pyramidal surfaces also represent sacred geometry as well as a form of record keeping. Mystery School meditation with sacred geometry can help the individual reawaken their body and nervous system to that of higher consciousness. As Hunbatz Men says, "Information is stored in stone and bone." We can connect with that higher information in these sacred sites that hold that information.

Each site may have different guardians or spirit keepers who protect the site but also assist appropriate, respectful seekers. When asked for help they may help the individual bring information held at that site into their nervous system, which affects change and evolution.

The information available at these sites is not limited to any one group or Mystery School. It is truly ancient and beyond time. The New Age is really a return to Cosmic Consciousness. An opportunity to reconnect with that that is greater then the small Self, the separate Self, the Ego.

Wouldn't you like to be reconnected to Cosmic Consciousness, to Cosmic Wisdom?"

Ricardo's Notes:

The other way to teach our own bodies' energy field to vibrate along with that of mother earth is to practice the Omkabah Heart Lightbody activation with ancient enlightenment Qigong forms that open the heart to unconditional love and develop the energy bubbles of Qigong practitioners. Doing the Omkabah Lightbody activation with enlightenment Qigong forms at the sacred sites like the pyramids of Egypt, the Sphinx, the Mayan Pyramids, Stonehenge, Mesa Verde, etc. strongly change our energy vibration fields and reconnect the Qigong practitioners to Cosmic Consciousness, to Cosmic Wisdom.

As one of the Enlightenment Qigong forms that reconnect to Cosmic Consciousness, the Maitreya Shen Gong practice will assist your energy field to make the vibrational shift in 2012 and beyond to synchronize with the vibrational shift of Mother Earth's light grid.

Conclusion

Acharya Ricardo's Notes:

According to Tyberonn of Earth-Keeper.com, "The ascension grid (aka Light-grid) is the newly formed energetic lattice that covers our planet. It reflects and amplifies our ascending levels of consciousness... The concept of planetary grid is not a new one. Plato theorized the concept as did the ancient Egyptians, Mayans and Hopi Indians. In a sense, grids are the template, the program, that allows all life to operate in the graduated light format. If you will, the Ascension Grid, is 'Windows 2012', and it is quite necessary for our ascension."

From the above explanation by Tyberonn on the ascension grid with its activation, Maitreya Shen Gong is done in great part for Maitreya's loving energy and Solar God Orion belt connection, transferral and activation of the ascension grid, the crystal matrix or kundalini of Gaia (serpent of light), and planetary Logos or planetary God. In return we strengthen, activate and expand our merkaba field (lightbody) and experience enlightenment -- the blissful awakening of our Buddha Nature through Heaven, Humanity and Earth Qigong.

The Omkabah Heart Lightbody Activation together with Maitreya Shen Gong or other Enlightenment Qigong forms draw into your heart from the heavenly energy from the heart of the Father Source – Orion belt and Sun, and from the kundalini energy from the heart center of Mother Earth. If you cannot visit the sacred sites, you can visualize yourself meditating or doing Qigong in the sacred sites to gather the kundalini energy from the sites to develop your merkaba (energy bubble or electromagnetic field).

"The Hologram of Love Merkaba is our doorway home." ~ Alton Kamadon

Merkaba activation is best integrated with the Qigong forms such as Maitreya (Shiva) Shen Gong taught at the Qigong workshops to build the Ka, pranic or energy body, and life-force (Qi), to open one's heart to the divine energy of unconditional love, to rewire and gradually develop the capacity of the body's Qi circuitry (meridians and 8 extraordinary meridians) and higher subtle bodies to absorb minute dosages of intense divine energy, and gradually strengthen the Qi connection and oneness with one's Higher Soul, the spiritual teachers, humanity, the universe (earth, sun, moon, planets and stars), and God.

"*Chanting trishakti shodashi mantra with Sarvayoni mudra result in the bliss of samadhi.*" – Acharya Ricardo B Serrano, *See Guruji Amritananda*, page 16; *Kundalini Shakti*, page 21; *Sri Yantra*, page 119

Love is. Love will always be. Love is eternity.

Rising Earth Kundalini (Serpent of Light) & Kundalini Awakening

An Introduction to Kundalini Awakening

The following revelations presented by Drunvalo Melchizedek from his book "Serpent of Light: Beyond 2012" made me realize the blissful spiritual awakening process – the rising of Earth's Kundalini (Serpent Of Light) that happens within and through me connecting with the Unity Consciousness Grid -- everytime I regularly practice breathing with postures, meditation and Qigong, especially the Maitreya (Shiva) Shen Gong with Omkabah Lightbody Activation and the integrated Enlightenment Qigong forms.

From what I understand from my studies on sacred geometry and merkaba with my late teacher Merkaba master Alton Kamadon, a Flower of Life student of Drunvalo Melchizedek, the earth's kundalini or serpent of light has now shifted its position on the surface of the earth in the Andes mountains in Chile and Peru. To verify this shift, I meditated etherically in that area and have felt a stronger connection with the electromagnetic field in the Andes mountains photos as a result of the rising kundalini energy there. Based on my said experience, I believe that what was told by Drunvalo Melchizedek regarding the vibrational energy shift of the serpent of light in the Andes mountains from his book "Serpent of Light: Beyond 2012" is true.

The earth kundalini energy is called the Serpent of Light or called the Great White Snake in other Oriental traditions. Not only is the earth's kundalini energy very similar to a human being's, but also even such massive energy fields as the merkaba field of the planet and the human merkaba field (light body) are exactly the same except for proportional size. The earth's kundalini energy connected to the center of the earth behaves like a snake as it moves, similar to the way kundalini energy moves in the human body which is the secret energy, the inner Shakti, that gives rise to the kundalini awakening of spiritual seekers everywhere on earth.

Because the vast influence of the earth's kundalini energy or Serpent of Light in the sacred sites in Tibet and India inevitably affected greatly the bodies, minds and hearts of people who lived around its vicinity, it gave birth to the great souls and spiritual teachers such as Lao Tzu, the author of Tao Te Ching (The Way of the Tao), and the Buddha, the founder of Buddhism, a world religion that has a deeper understanding of the human electromagnetic energy fields and higher consciousness.

The key, I believe, based on the experience and accomplishment of the great spiritual teachers from Tibet and India who thrived from the enlightening energy of the serpent of light for spiritual transformation, is to develop our energy bubble (electromagnetic field) by practicing meditation and Qigong in the sacred sites strengthening and connecting our energy bubble with the strong electromagnetic fields of the sacred areas which are dependent on the earth's rising kundalini energy in the sacred site.

What this means also is that the end of the Mayan calendar has a positive benefit in the spiritual transformation for planet earth with its masses of people because of a stronger flow of earth's kundalini energy in the sacred sites such as the pyramids and other areas on the earth's surface that are easily accessible for power journeys to spiritual seekers.

Despite the doom and gloom scenarios depicted by unawakened persons regarding the end of Mayan calendar, I believe the opposite is true that is vitally important for our survival with the help of mother earth and her serpent of light -- an important sacred event which starts the spiritual transformation of planet earth and her people at the beginning of 2013 -- the end of the reign of the little self (ego mind) and the recognition of the formless being that we truly are.

Because the Truth can only be known by experience, not by beliefs or thoughts as Master Jesus said "And you will know the Truth and the Truth will set you free," and in light of what was revealed here -- the kundalini energy of sacred sites is a portal to presence -- the most important question is "What are you going to do to experience the Truth, now?"

"Nothing Changes Until You Get Moving towards Unconditional Love!"

By linking your heart to the source of Father God and to the heart center of Mother Earth allows you to draw the spiritual energies of God source and Earth together to manifest a high frequency unconditional love healing energy that uplifts the human body and etheric bodies into a state of receptivity for spiritual ascension, healing and rejuvenation.

According to Drunvalo, "You ask what you can do? Easy -- leave your mind and your constant thoughts and return to your heart. Inside your heart is a tiny place where all knowledge and wisdom resides. Whatever you need on all levels of your existence is there for you.

And, in the human and earthly changes that we are surrounded by, and the incredible changes that are about to permeate our everyday lives, if you are living in your heart, Mother Earth will take care of you with her soft magical love, the same magical love that created this entire physical planet in the first place.

Remember who you really are, trust yourself, and open your eyes to the new beauty of a new Earth unfolding before you as we breathe. Peer past the darkness and destruction of the ending of this old male cycle. Do not look into Kali's eyes. But put your attention on the budding life and light in the center of the vortex.

Like a seed, your future is only beginning to emerge out of the darkness, but someday you will look back and realize that all the fear and distress was only a dream created from the confusion of the ending of one cycle and the beginning of another. Death and life are part of the same cycle. See *Kundalini Shakti (Sri Devi)*, page 21

Guruji Amritananda Natha Saraswati is Acharya Ricardo B Serrano's Guru. See *Kundalini Shakti*, page 21; *Sri Yantra* page 119; Guruji Quotes, page 135

Lalitha Tripura Sundari

Aeem Hreem Shreem Aeem Kleem Sauh

Now, look into the Light and breathe deeply the joy of life. Eternal Life without suffering was yours all along. Never were you ever separated from the Source. Live your life without fear. Live your life with open eyes and an open heart from the jewel within your heart, and you will extend yourself into the next 13,000 years here on Earth and far, far beyond."

> OM MANI PADME HUM OM MANI PADME HUM OM MANI PADME HUM
>
> Behold! The Jewel in the Lotus!

Excerpted from Serpent of Light: Beyond 2012 by Drunvalo Melchizedek, 2008.

Every 13,000 years on Earth a sacred and secret event takes place that changes everything. Mother Earth's Kundalini energy emerges from its resting place in the planet's core and moves like a snake across the surface of our world. Once at home in ancient Lemuria, it moved to Atlantis, then to the Himalayan mountains of India and Tibet, and with every relocation changed our idea of what spiritual means. And gender. And heart.

This time, with much difficulty, the "Serpent of Light" has moved to the Andes Mountains of Chile and Peru. Multi-dimensional, multi-disciplined and multi- lived, for the first time in this book, Drunvalo begins to tell his stories of 35 years spent in service to Mother Earth. Follow him around the world as he follows the guidance of Ascended Masters, his two spheres of light, and his own inner growing knowledge.

His story is a living string of ceremonies to help heal hearts, align energies, right ancient imbalances, and balance the living Earth's Unity Consciousness Grid -- in short to increase our awareness of the indivisibility of life in the universe. We are all -- rocks and people and interdimensional beings -- one!

"Life may seem to be business as usual, but it is not. We are changing fast
...Remember this for life is going to present stranger things to you in your lifetime, and they all have meaning and purpose ...Only Mother Earth and ancient Maya know what's going to happen."

Serpent of Light Beyond 2012
by Drunvalo Melchizedek

"The Serpent of Light has moved to the Andes Mountains of Chile and Peru." ~ Drunvalo Melchizedek

Introduction

Life is amazing! Every 13,000 years on Earth a sacred and secret event takes place that changes everything, an event that changes the very course of history. At this moment, this rare event is occurring, but only a few people know. Most of those who do know have kept it quiet and hidden until now.

What I am speaking about is the Earth's Kundalini. Connected to the center of the Earth is an energy that appears and behaves much like a snake as it moves, similar to the way Kundalini energy moves in the human body.

It is this energy that gives rise to spiritual seekers everywhere on Earth ... not only in the ashrams, kankas and monasteries of the world, but also even in ordinary life and ordinary people who, in their own way, are seeking Goddess. The Earth's Kundalini is the secret energy that is connected to the hearts of all of humankind.

The Earth's Kundalini is always attached to a single location on the surface of the Earth and stays there for a period of about 13,000 years. Then it moves on to a new location for the next 13,000 years, based upon cycles of 9, or what we call the Precession of the Equinox. When it moves, our idea of what "Spiritual" means changes. It transforms according to the new energies of the future cycle leading us into a higher spiritual path.

The bigger picture is this. The Kundalini has two poles, and one is in the exact center of the Earth. The other is located on the surface somewhere and anywhere in the world. It is the consciousness of the Earth herself that decides where it is to be.

There is a pulse of exactly 12,920 years when the polarity of the Earth's Kundalini changes to the opposite pole, and it simultaneously changes location on the surface of the Earth. This new location not only rapidly wakes up the people living near this sacred point on Earth, but also sends a frequency into the electromagnetic grids surrounding the Earth. This in turn, affects those consciousness grids in ways that are determined by the Earth's DNA. We grow according to a set plan and design!

To the few that know of this event and what is occurring all around us, a wisdom is transferred, and a peaceful state of being becomes their inheritance, for they know the awesome truth. In the midst of chaos, war, starvation, plagues, environmental crisis and moral breakdown that we are experiencing here on Earth today at the end of this cycle, they understand the transition and know no fear. This fearless state is the secret key to the transformation that, for millions of years, has always followed this sacred cosmic event.

On one level this means that spiritually the Female will now have her turn to lead humankind into the New Light! Eventually, this Female spiritual light will permeate the entire range of human experience from Female leaders in business and religion to Female heads of state. By 2012-2013 this Female spiritual light will become so strong as to become obvious to all who live on this dear planet and will continue to grow for thousands of years.

For many of you, none of this will probably make any sense until you read chapters 2 and 3. Chapter 2 is the Cosmic Knowledge of what is actually occurring in nature and in the stars and how it relates to this new cycle of light. Chapter 3 is the history of what the ancient cultures understood about this sacred event up to this present time. This prepares you for the content of this book.

Beginning with Chapter 4 will be the stories of my personal experience and involvement with this "Serpent of Light" and the hundreds of indigenous tribes/cultures that have secretly helped guide this spiritual energy from Tibet to its new home in South America! Coming out of Tibet into India, it then moved in a snakelike manner to almost every country in the world until it reached Chile, the new home of the Earth's Kundalini, the new "Tibet".

What has occurred in the world along this path that the Earth's Kundalini has taken has been almost unbelievable. People from different cultures and countries all cooperating together "as though" they were coordinated by a higher power simply for the good of human life. Without this spiritual assistance, I believe, humanity will be unable to evolve to the next level of consciousness, crucial to our very survival.

For me, the call to this way of life was so strong that I felt like I had no choice. It simply began to happen all around me as I followed my inner-guidance.

But I am not the only one. There are tens or thousands of people, mostly indigenous people, who have been led by a deep inner guidance, from 1949 to the present, to help bring this unyielding White Snake to its new location high up in the Andes Mountains in Chile, where it now finally resides. Not only is this a shift of spiritual power from the male to Female, but it is also a spiritual power shift from Tibet and India to Chile and Peru. The Light of the World that has been nurtured and expanded with the Tibetan and Indian cultures is now completed. Its new reign has just begun in Chile and Peru, and soon it will affect the hearts of all humankind.

These are my personal stories as I have followed my inner-guidance helping bring balance to a troubled world. My training has been to stay connected with Mother Earth and Father Sky within a secret place within my heart. It is very simple. Once one is connected to the Divine Mother and Father in this way, life becomes one miracle after another. Never could anyone plan these kinds of stories. They are conceived from outside myself in the nature that surrounds us. Some of these stories break the laws of physics, but not the laws of our Mother.

Like I said, Life is amazing! Drunvalo

Kundalini Shakti (Sri Devi)

According to my Sri Vidya Guru, *Sri Amritananda Natha Saraswati*, Sri Devi: Hindus call her Gayatri, Christians call her the Virgin Mary, Buddhists call her the Compassion, Sufis call her the Movement; other ancient religions simply call her Mother Earth. She is our source, our sustenance and our end. She is Kundalini, the power moving us toward the unity of all life.

These are Her two poles; She is the bipolar entity, the unity of opposites. And the world manifests in the separation of Kali and Kala; it disappears in their union.

She combines in Herself the tenderness of all mothers and the passion of all lovers, wisdom and insanity, childishness and experience, cruelty and faithfulness.

She is maya; dissolution of maya leads to mahasamadhi from which there is no return. This is the reason why it is insisted that you treat Devi as your mother; then the thought of enjoying Her does not arise that easily in the head, preserving your life. But think! what better way to die than in the hands of mother, to become Shiva, a death like corpse? If you are Her child, She feeds you with milk from Her ever full breasts; and the milk of life is sweet indeed. But in the total recognition there is no second – one does indeed become Shiva and Shakti in union; then there is no manifest world, except the continuous unending bliss. And one who has once tasted the sweetness of it, does not want to come back, except as a sacrifice of freedom brought about willfully!

So long you have been sleeping under delusion; now that you have already known the nature of your own self by the grace of Guru, then why yet to hesitate? By leaving aside all your idleness and giving up all sorts of your weakness, raise up yourself, and with the shouting of 'DEVI', 'DEVI', awaken Her Dears from their sleep!

See *Guruji Amritananda Natha Saraswati*, page 16; *Sri Yantra*, page 119; *Guruji Quotes*, page 135

Hologram of Love Merkaba according to Alton Kamadon

According to Merkaba Master Alton Kamadon, "The hologram of love (Merkaba) is the sacred geometric pattern which gave birth to the whole universe. It is based on unconditional love, so it must be the pattern of unconditional love, because everything in the universe resonates to it, no matter what it is or what dimension it's in. That means that you and I, as human beings, also have that pattern within us, so we are actually walking, talking unconditional love. We always have been, we've just never recognized it.

However, you can't really measure this in third dimensional terms. This is a high concept of divine creation that you intuitively resonate to. It's not something to be analyzed by the left brain. Those who are drawn to this intuitively find that, as soon as they apply it, they have the most extraordinary experiences and their whole body changes. They meditate in a way that activates the Holographic Merkaba with light, invoking a special frequency of 13:20:33 into that field of continuous time.

What is this 13:20:33 frequency? Part of what we came to learn as human beings was how to live with limitation, and the 12:60 timing that we have allowed ourselves to be encompassed within is a timing of limitation. It was brought in through the Gregorian calendar, and represents the 12 months of the year, the 60 minutes in the hour, etc. I work with a different frequency -- 13:20:33 -- a frequency of no limitation. If you study the human body, you will find that this frequency is harmonized through it. We have 13 major articulations in the body -- ankles, knees, hips, wrists, elbows, shoulders and the neck -- and 20 fingers and toes. When you add 20 and 13, you arrive at the master number of 33, which is also the number of vertebrae in the spine -- the center of the body. The ancient Mayans used the frequency of 13 and 20 for their calendar of time, awakened God Consciousness within themselves, and enabled them to access the center of the universe and merge with it. The process provides a spherical perspective called omni perspective which, in turn, helps individuals live in non-judgement and to be the witness in our illusionary physical world. They thus become galactically aligned and empowered.

How is this frequency applied? If our ultimate goal is to merge back with God, then God our Creator made our bodies to transcend this physical world by providing keys and formulas within us to achieve this. When you relate this key to the hologram of love, you'll see that those two concepts together make up the ultimate key to ascension. The frequency of 13:20:33 is the frequency of no time. The hologram of love is symbolic of the time continuum because it's all made up of curves. When you try to measure linear time, or anything in this world, it has straight edges or angles. But when we work with the hologram of love, we are working with the curves of continuous time. You look at that design and see that it goes into itself continuously, circle after circle. When you put it into a hologram, you end up with sphere after sphere, and there is no beginning or end. That is the pattern of our human body. If you put those two things together -- 13:20:33 and the Hologram of Love (utilizing the curves of time) -- you can create a whole new body form and consciousness.

What exactly is the time/space continuum? As we make our transition into our light body or form of creation, we withdraw from linear time (measured in a straight line, with a beginning and an end), and we move into the time continuum, which is timeless spiritual existence, with no beginning or end. According to the Egyptian spirit guide Thoth, the time/space continuum is attached to the spine. This makes it very easy to withdraw yourself from your physical body within a meditation through your own time/space continuum. Thoth teaches us that we are already in unity consciousness - and always have been - and it's a complete illusion that we are not, because we are always attached to God through the time/space continuum and always have been. We have just not allowed ourselves the expansion of consciousness to accept there is something else (the time continuum) that is part of our body.

In practical terms, what can the hologram of love do for people? First of all, it will open up their psychic abilities through their pineal gland. It will activate a rotational field of life that encompasses this dimension and all the others beyond us. It also provides a completely different perception of creation, expanding consciousness, and exerting an amazing effect on your heart. As soon as you use the hologram of love, it activates the love center, and opens up your heart spontaneously, so that you can express and receive much more love. You can also use this technique to heal yourself permanently.

What about a degenerative condition caused by poor diet, for example? You are working with holograms which are thought-induced. If you work with the time/space continuum of the hologram of love, you immediately change the timing around the physical body. In other words, your physical self resonates to a 12:60 illusionary memory. Now if you use this other concept, you change the memory of the cell and you bring it into the time/space continuum where everything is perfect. It is only down at this third-dimensional level that we have imperfection.

What's marvelous about this is that if a person has created an illness through incorrect eating, and the illness is healed with this particular technique, this changes the thought pattern in the person so that they then begin to change their diet. It happens automatically, changing the memory cell. This is what makes this process so extraordinary. We're talking about permanent changes in people -- not something that will re-manifest.

Can you give some example of that? I have worked with two cancer cases recently, both of which were totally healed in a relatively short period of time. They were treated with 30-minute sessions for five days, until the cancer was completely gone. One individual, with cervical cancer, felt as if her insides were being sucked out of her. This was all done with the hologram and thought, with no other modalities used. There are many different hologram modalities out there, but none of them use this particular pattern and frequency which are the key to the permanent and total healing achieved with this approach. Anyone can do this. It's a three-breath activation, very quick and extremely effective. The energy in this hologram of love is much more refined -- as it should be, as a higher vibration beyond the third dimension. The simplest form can be learnt by anyone within an hour or less. Once the hologram is activated and locked into your heart, it becomes part of you, breathing with you, and is very soft and malleable, like an outer skin. Once it's there, we simply take one focused breath and it is immediately re-activated. You just have to think about it, and you see and feel it.

According to Thoth, unconditional love is a powerful magnetic force which, once activated through the hologram of love, makes you truly magnetic within every cell of your body. As a result, you begin to attract all you need to become a cosmic vibration of higher wisdom. If we could understand time and love together, Thoth said, we would have the answer."

Thoth has had quite a few incarnations on Earth. He is also known through his work during his incarnations as Chiquetet Arlich Vomilities in Atlantean life time, and as Hermes Trismegistus in Ancient Greece. Each time he has appeared he has had a significant impact on the cultures of humankind on Earth.

Merkaba is an interdimensional counterclockwise rotational vehicle of Light, Pranic or energy body and Soul. Mer - counterclockwise rotation of Light, ka - Pranic or energy body, ba - Soul. The mind directs, powers, and stabilises the Merkaba in unison with God. The higher your vibration of Cosmic Christ Consciousness embraced in Unconditional love, the stronger is your Merkaba field. The Merkaba is the chosen interdimensional vehicle of the Masters. To truly extend ourselves into their conscious realms we must raise the vibration of Love within our personal Merkaba. The Hologram of Love is the ever continuous pattern of God's mind and thought because God only thinks and manifests in unconditional Love. The Hologram of Love Merkaba meditation accesses the unified field of consciousness through the galactic timing of the universe.

Quotations on the Flower of Life Hologram of Love

The Flower of Life Hologram of Love is the sacred symbol of unconditional love. All the elements represented by sacred geometrical shapes (Fire - star tetrahedron, Air - octahedron, Earth - cube, Water - icosahedron, and Ether - dodecahedron) are within the Flower of Life. The whole universe was born through this sacred sphere. Your RNA/DNA was born through this holographic flower of life pattern. The finest particle of our atomic cell structure has this pattern within it.

Merkaba meditation techniques are included in the Maitreya (Shiva) Shen Gong practice for spiritual empowerment (Shaktipat), lightbody activation, holographic healing, opening one's heart to unconditional love, spiritual ascension and enhance "being in the flow of Qi" and "Qi-healing" a 100-fold.

The basis of the techniques is the activation of the Hologram of Love Merkaba, a rotating lightfield awakening your spherical consciousness. This will actually raise one's quotient of light vibration within the human atomic cell structure. Once activated, the merkaba assists us in accessing our natural Qigong state of ascended consciousness. The heart awakens and opens more to unconditional love during healing sessions and this opening continues during your normal life. The tool of the Hologram of Love is a high dimensional Divine manifestation of living that allows one to access all levels of consciousness. It has the ability to heal and rejuvenate any form of creation as it is the living conscious holographic pattern of God Source vibration.

Linking your heart to the source of Father God and to the heart center of Mother Earth allows you to draw the spiritual energies of God source and Earth together to manifest a high frequency love healing energy that uplifts the human body and etheric bodies into a state of receptivity for spiritual ascension, healing and rejuvenation.

"Divine light vehicle used by the Masters to probe and reach the faithful in the many dimensions of the Divine Mind. The Merkabah can take on many forms of a brilliant briolette in the physical worlds." -- J.J.Hurtak, Keys of Enoch

"The key to future luminaries and the key to the "divine light" is the vehicle of time translation. The "vehicle of vehicles" is "Merkabah" which creates, controls, and has the ability "to speak" through electromagnetic sinks. Merkabah revolves and goes, and rises under the heaven, or brightness of the next universe, and its course goes over the earth with the "light of its rays" incessantly into myriads of universes within the ever unfolding eternity." -- Keys of Enoch 3-0-1

Divine Eye of God

Visualise yourself sitting within the center of the Omkabah within the all-knowing, all-seeing divine Eye of God, with the Layooesh pillar of light connected to your spine. You are the center of this lightbody structure.

In this greater universe the Elohim recreate life with light encodement vibrations from the eternal eye. The eternal divine eye of God holds all the light encodements for the divine creation of multiple bodies of light. As one enters through the eternal divine eye of God you chant the holy mantras 3X:

METATRON – LAY-OO-ESH – AMEN-P'TAAH
PHOWA – QUAN YIN – GABRIEL - BUDDHA
KODOISH KODOISH KODOISH ADONAI T'SEBAYOTH
I AM THAT I AM – EHYEH ASHER EHYEH

It expresses the covenant between the human self and the Christed overself with a knowing of one's identity and destiny with the encodements to the higher worlds of light. It is also a holy mantra/salutation working with the White Brotherhoods and the heirarchy of YHWH.

Kodoish Kodoish Kodoish Adonai Tsebayoth means Holy Holy Holy is the Lord God of Hosts. It is a universal greeting of the lightworkers of universal energy, and is used for protection.

It is also a cosmic vibration that unites the lower I AM to the higher I AM to stimulate our spiritual growth through divine love.

Our biological clock heartbeat is set to the vibration frequency of this holy mantra uniting the biorhythms of the physical to the spiritual vibrational frequency of the overself of our highest superconscious mind.

The Kodoish Kodoish Kodoish Adonai Tsebayoth assists in the direct vibratory conscious connection to the Elohim Creator Lords of Light in Orionis.

When this holy mantra Kodoish Kodoish Kodoish Adonai Tsebayoth is chanted with the Omkabah lightbody spin rotation, an harmonic resonance is created connecting your lower Adamic seed pattern to your higher Adamic seed pattern within the creative source of God which automatically repels all negative forces that cannot remain in the presence of its vibration.

Chant the GAYATRI mantra (3x) , OM MANI PADME HUM (3X), Heart Sutra (3x) and VAJRA GURU mantra (3x) visualising the sound vibration continuously resonating through your Omkabah, and expanding into all the universes;

GAYATRI

OM BHUR BUVA SWAHA TAT SAVITUR VARENYAM BHARGO DEVASYA DHEEMAHI DHIYO YO NAH PRACHODAYAT OM . . . SHANTI . . . SHANTI . . . SHANTIHI	We meditate on the glory of that Being who has created this universe . . who is to be worshipped . . . who is the remover of all sins and ignorance. May he enlighten our intellect.
OM MANI PADME HUM OM MANI PADME HUM OM MANI PADME HUM	Behold! The Jewel in the Lotus (The jewel is within your heart)
[OM] GATE GATE PARAGATE PARASAMGATE BODHI SVAHA	GONE, GONE, GONE BEYOND, COMPLETELY GONE BEYOND, ENLIGHTENMENT, HAIL
OM AH HUM VAJRA GURU PADMA SIDDHI HUM	I invoke you, the Vajra Guru, Padmasambhava, by your blessing may you grant us ordinary and supreme siddhis.

The Heart of Prajna Paramita Sutra

When Avalokiteshvara Bodhisattva was practicing the profound prajna paramita, he illuminated the five skandhas and saw that they are all empty, and he crossed beyond all suffering and difficulty.

Shariputra, form does not differ from emptiness; emptiness does not differ from form. Form itself is emptiness; emptiness itself is form. So, too, are feeling, cognition, formation, and consciousness.

Shariputra, all dharmas are empty of characteristics. They are not produced. Not destroyed, not defiled, not pure, and they neither increase or diminish. Therefore, in emptiness there is no form, feeling, cognition, formation, or consciousness; no eyes, ears, nose, tongue, body, or mind; no sights, sounds, smells, tastes, objects of touch, or dharmas; no field of the eyes, up to and including no field of mind-consciousness; and no ignorance or ending of ignorance, up to and including no old age and death or ending of old age and death. There is no suffering, no accumulating, no extinction, no way, and no understanding and no attaining.

Because nothing is attained, the Bodhisattva, through reliance on prajna paramita, is unimpeded in his mind. Because there is no impediment, he is not afraid, and he leaves distorted dream-thinking far behind. Ultimately Nirvana!

All Buddhas of the three periods of time attain Anuttarasamyaksambodhi through reliance on prajna paramita. Therefore, know that prajna paramita is a great spiritual mantra, a great bright mantra, a supreme mantra, an unequalled mantra. It can remove all suffering; it is genuine and not false. That is why the mantra of prajna paramita was spoken. Recite it like this:

[OM] GATE GATE PARAGATE PARASAMGATE BODHI SVAHA !(3X)
(GONE, GONE, GONE BEYOND, COMPLETELY GONE BEYOND, ENLIGHTENMENT, HAIL)

Heart Sutra Commentary:

Buddha illuminated the five skandhas and saw that they are all empty.

Verse:

The three lights shine everywhere,
permeating the three forces.
The one returns to the place of union,
yet the one comes forth again.
See that form is emptiness
and that feeling is the same way;
False thoughts are the shifting currents,
while formation is the arranger of karma;
With consciousness, which understands differences,
the five shadows are completed.
Mirror-flowers and water-moon,
beyond defiling dust:
Emptiness not empty – the great function of clarity;
Vision is yet not a view – happiness indeed!

The three lights shine everywhere, permeating the three forces. "The three lights" are the sun, the moon, and the stars, which illuminate everything in the universe and thoroughly penetrate "the three forces" of heaven, earth, and humanity. The three lights are also the lights of wisdom: the light of the prajna of language, the light of the prajna of contemplative illumination, and the light of the prajna of the characteristic of actuality (The three are also said to be the symbolic red, white, and purple lights). The light of true prajna of the characteristic of actuality is the very deep prajna-light by which Avalokiteshvara Bodhisattva illuminated the five skandhas and saw that they are all empty. With the three kinds of light he illuminates every place in the heavens and on earth, and the lights permeate the three motive forces.

The one returns to the place of union, yet the one comes forth again. "The one" refers to one's own nature. The "place of union" is where one's own nature dwells. Basically it is this: "Ten thousand dharmas return to one; one returns to unity."

* Heart of Prajna Paramita Sutra by Venerable Tripitaka Master Hsuan Hua, 2002.

Kundalini Awakening in the Mayan Pyramids

The power journeys with Ricardo B Serrano, a Toltec mentor and Qigong master, are about the spiritual and healing benefits derived by his Toltec friends who have journeyed in the ancient megalithic sites at Teotihuacan, Chichen Itza, Mexico, and Machu Picchu.

The following quotes from Mayan elder Hunbatz Men elaborate the cosmic principles behind the kundalini awakening that Toltec and Mayan practitioners experience during their power journeys at the pyramid of Kukulcan, the pyramids such as the Great Pyramid at Gizah, Egypt, the pyramids at the Teotihuacan complex, Machu Picchu, and other sacred sites:

According to Hunbatz Men' book Secrets of Mayan Science and Religion, Men expands on the meaning of the Kukulcan archetype. He explains that "Ku" means sacred, God. "Kul" is coccyx, the base of the spine where a mysterious solar charge resides. "Can" means serpent. "Kukulcan" therefore, is the serpent of sacred knowledge -- virtually one and the same as kundalini, fiery serpent energy of Eastern yoga traditions. This same serpent energy is known in esoteric yoga traditions throughout Mesoamerica and is commonly referred to by its Aztec name Quetzalcoatl, or Feathered Serpent.

Sacred knowledge associated with Feathered Serpent, Quetzalcoatl, is embedded in ancient pyramids throughout Mesoamerica. Thousands of people visit these structures each year but only a handful realize something very essential about them. It is a message conveyed on the lips of contemporary practitioners of Mayan spirituality when they say: "You are the pyramid, the pyramid is you." What these practitioners are referring to is that the cosmic principles coded into sacred pyramid architecture are one and the same as those coded into the human body.

"The Mayan masters teach that we are the integration of the seven powers of light, traveling in the form of the serpent, undulating eternally with movement and measure. In Mayan, the pyramid is called k'u, the root word for the sacred Hunab K'u, the Only Giver of Movement and Measure. Thus, when we see the seven triangles in Chichen Itza during the equinoxes, we are witnessing a demonstration of culture which pervades the atmosphere and stones of this sacred place. With respect and humility, we should kneel before the presence of Kukulcan or Quetzalcoatl. By so doing, we will begin to awaken our cosmic consciousness, allowing Hunab K'u to enter the sacred temples in our bodies!" -- Hunbatz Men, Secrets of Mayan Science and Religion p.126

"There are several mysteries about the grand city (Teotihuacan) and its pyramids. One of the most interesting concerns the massive, one-foot thick, sheet of granulated mica that until recently covered the entire top level of the Pyramid of the Sun. Removed and sold for profit by an unscrupulous site-restorer in the early 1900's, the mica had long ago been transported from a mine thousands of miles away in South America. How had the great quantity of mica been brought from such a distance and, equally important, for what purpose had the pyramid been covered with the rare stone? One scientist has suggested that the mica, being a highly efficient energy conductor, could have been used as part of a receiving device for long wavelength celestial radiations. The incoming celestial energy would have been captured by the massive bulk of the pyramid and its sacred geometrical construction, and focused into the snake-like cave beneath the pyramid. This energy, available for human use at any time of the year, would be specially concentrated at certain periods within solar, lunar, and stellar cycles. These specific periods were noted by using astronomical observation devices that exist in different places around the geometrically aligned city of Teotihuacan." -- A Magical Mystery Tour of Teo

- "As with many other sacred spots around the world, Teotihuacan (Teo) combines unique geographic features, sources of spiritual energy, and a tradition of esoteric work by thousands of people over thousands of years. Visitors from all spiritual traditions gain inspiration and feel powerful energy from the pyramids and centers of spiritual study located throughout the huge site. Some use the symbolism of specific locations around the site to facilitate their process of transformation." –Teotihuacan
- According to the book Beyond Fear, "Fundamental to don Miguel's teachings is the concept that earthly life is hell. Hell is the combined dream that all humans share. Both individually and collective dreams are actually nightmares. Every individual has a dream of reality, and likewise, so does each family, each community, city, state, nation and the whole of humanity. We all contribute to the dream that is characterized by fear.

An ultimate healing would mean to awaken from the dream and to thereby be liberated from hell. Teotihuacan was designed for this purpose, to free humans from their fears. Such freedom restores the knowledge that humans are of a divine nature. They are gods. This is the source of the name -- Teotihuacan, which means, literally, "the Place Where Men Become Gods." Seekers of the Toltec way to freedom and joy follow a ritual procession along the main passageway in Teotihuacan as they move beyond fear into a state of empowerment."

Maitreya (Shiva) Shen Gong

"Maitreya Shen Gong practice will assist your energy field to make the vibrational shift in 2012 and beyond to synchronize with the vibrational shift of Mother Earth's light grid." ~ Ricardo B Serrano

The nine seated movements with contemplations of Maitreya (Shiva) sitting Qigong, an advance Tantric, Therapeutic, Earth and Heaven Qigong form, open the heart to unconditional love and clarify or dissolve the karmic layers in one's energy bubble (light body) resulting in enlightenment and experience of the Buddha Nature.

Maitreya (Shiva) sitting Qigong, a Shen Gong spiritual practice that is dedicated to self-realization and awakening of Buddha Nature, generates a tremendous downpouring of spiritual Light, Love and Power. You can use these divine energies for healing yourself and others. You can also use the divine energies for blessing humanity with loving-kindness, the essence of bodhicitta and the attitude of the bodhisattva.

Because Acharya Ricardo has been greatly transformed after an intense heart-opening spiritual unity experience with the universal love energy that is Maitreya through the regular practice of the nine seated movements of the Maitreya (Shiva) Shen Gong he developed naturally as his own authentic way to experience Buddha Nature, he has written the simple non-sectarian Shen Gong technology through his ebook for the benefit of everyone who want to experience inner peace and happiness, and as a form of world service by blessing with loving-kindness.

"The second coming of Christ (Maitreya) will be an enlightenment of the inner man."

"Your main savior is yourself."

"Maitreya will remain for 60,000 years, providing direct spiritual guidance to his many disciples during his lifetime and, after he passes away, his teachings will last another 80,000 years, indirectly benefiting many more. Thus, through the power of his great, enlightened loving-kindness, Maitreya will provide limitless benefit to countless mother sentient beings.

In the absolute sense Maitreya is subject to neither death nor rebirth; he is forever benefiting all mother sentient beings. Furthermore, he once declared, "Anybody keeping just one vow of moral discipline purely during the time of Shakyamuni Buddha's teachings will become my personal disciple when I appear and I shall liberate all such disciples," and he faithfully keeps this promise, his sworn oath and pledge.

Therefore, those of us fortunate enough to have met the teachings of Shakyamuni Buddha and maintained some level of pure discipline are guaranteed to make direct contact with Maitreya, become his disciple and quickly achieve enlightenment."

Lama Yeshe dedicated the merit of this translation as follows: "Because of this merit, may our life's energy be dedicated to the realization of Maitri-love, the actual nuclear weapon capable of destroying all external and internal enemies, just as Maitreya Buddha did, and may we reach the great state of equanimity, in which there are no neurotic friends, enemies or strangers."

Many religions believe in a coming World Teacher, knowing him under such names as Christ, Krishna, Lord Maitreya, Imam Mahdi, Bodhisattva, and Messiah. These terms are used everyday with Christian, Hindu, Muslim, Buddhist and Jewish versions of the Great Invocation.

From the point of Light within the Mind of God
Let light stream forth into the minds of men.
Let Light descend on Earth.

From the point of Love within the Heart of God
Let love stream forth into the hearts of men.
May the Christ return to Earth.

From the center where the Will of God is known
Let purpose guide the little wills of men.
The purpose which the Masters know and serve.

From the center which we call the race of men
Let the Plan of Love and Light work out.
And may it seal the door where evil dwells.

Let Light and Love and Power restore the Plan on Earth.

People of goodwill throughout the world are using this invocation daily in their own language. Join them in using the Great Invocation every day - with righteous intent, thought and dedication. Use this Invocation and encourage others to use it. No particular group or organisation is sponsored. It belongs to all humanity.

The Use of Qigong to Develop Your Energy Bubble (Lightbody)

Lamas and Qigong masters have demonstrated the use of Qigong to develop your Energy Bubble, Electromagnetic Field (EMF), or Lightbody by rooting down to earth's EMF when intented for self-defense, healing and enlightenment. As an integral system of Oriental medicine, Qigong is based on the coherence of human energy fields within the universal flow of Qi, or life force from heaven and earth accompanied with the blissful expanded sense of oneness and physical, mental, emotional and spiritual equanimity.

The practice of Zhan Zhuang Qigong aligns the body's EMF with the Earth's EMF and enables the body to root down, and increase our ability to induct and conduct this EM force. The longer, and the more you train, the stronger your electromagnetic field (EMF) gets. This is essentially how Lin Kong Jing, the empty force, manifests when called on for healing or self-defense.

The practice of Sheng Zhen Wuji Yuan Gong (or Wuji Qigong) aligns the body's EMF with the Earth's EMF and heaven's Tian Qi, spiritual divine energy, purifying the physical body, calming the emotional body, and opening the heart/ elevating the Spirit together with building the Three Treasures - Jing, Qi and Shen - developing the Energy Bubble (Lightbody) leading to whole body enlightenment, as opposed to head enlightenment taught by other popular yoga schools that cause negative after-effects of post kundalini syndromes.

The practice of Earth Qigong, illustrated in the Earth Qigong Logo, as an important component of the Enlightenment Qigong forms, accesses the Earth's "Di Qi" and energy body to develop and expand your energy body's connection with the Cosmic Christ (Buddhic) consciousness grid - the unified field of the planet's energy body and its consciousness together with universal consciousness. This is based on the principle of interconnectedness or oneness which states that we are interconnected with the whole cosmos (earth, sun, moon, solar system, stars) or universe and each other.

The practice of Heaven Qigong, illustrated in the Heaven Qigong picture, as another important component of the Enlightenment Qigong forms, replenishes the heaven's "Tian Qi" or spiritual divine energy to develop strong internal Qi, especially when fused with the Earth's "Di Qi" derived from Earth Qigong practice. Healing and enlightenment are made possible through the awakening of the kundalini by opening and activation of the 5 energy gateways - crown of the head, palms of the hands, and soles of the feet - by the combined practice of Heaven and Earth Qigong in the ancient heart opening lineage Enlightenment Qigong Forms.

"Spiritual energy is needed for expansion of consciousness and traveling in the inner worlds. Stillness and awareness are not enough. No spiritual energy, no expansion of consciousness." -- Sutra 10 from MCKS The Existence of God is Self-Evident

Through the practice of Enlightenment Qigong forms such as Pan Gu Shengong, Primordial Wuji Qigong, Sheng Zhen Qigong and Maitreya sitting Qigong together with Tibetan Shamanic Qigong, the body and mind become very calm. This state of peace allows the heart to open to its natural state of unconditional love. The unconditional love (Sheng Zhen) of the universe floods into and out of the heart of the practitioner, producing a state of wholeness, of oneness with All. When one arrives at this altered Qigong state, there is a sense of merging with everything everywhere. The practitioner returns to his natural state, a state of perfect well-being.

The Tao that can be spoken of is not the eternal Tao;
The name that can be named is not the eternal name.
The nameless is the origin of Heaven and Earth;
The named is the root of all things.
Ever desireless, one can see the mystery.
Ever desiring, one can see the manifestations.
These two spring from the same source but differ in name;
this appears as darkness.
Darkness within darkness.
The gate to all mystery.

Chapter One in Tao Te Ching

WHO AM I?

"We are all children of God. In each person, there is a divine essence or a divine spark. In Buddhism, there is a Buddha in each person. In Christian religion, there is a Christ in each person. In Hinduism, there is a Shiva or a Krishna in each person.

What is the name of this divine essence? When Moses saw the burning bush, he asked, "If the people ask me what is your name, what shall I tell them?" From within the burning bush God answered, "I AM THAT I AM." (Exodus 3:13-14) In Hebrew, this is called Eieh. In Sanskrit, this is known as So Ham or Tatwamasi. There is a universal or planetary I AM. There is a micro I AM in every person.

Jesus says in John 14:6, "I AM the way and the truth and the life. No one comes to the Father except through me." Does Jesus literally mean that he is the way, the truth and the life, or does he mean that the I AM or higher soul within you is the way, the truth and the life? Does Jesus mean himself as the way to the Father or is this a reference to the I AM or higher soul within every person? "The Divine Father" here refers to the divine spark in every person.

The divine spark in every person is a part of God. It is made in the essence of God. The divine spark is one with God and one with all. The divine spark extends a portion of itself "downward", manifesting as the higher soul. The higher soul extends a portion of itself "downward", manifesting as the incarnated soul. In Hindu teachings, the incarnated soul is called Jivatma. It literally means "embodied soul." The higher soul is called Atma. The divine spark is called Paramatma. This is why St. Paul said that you have a body, soul, and spirit (1 Thessalonians 5:23). Here, "spirit" refers to the divine spark in each person. To achieve union with the divine spark or the Divine Father within you, you must first pass through the I AM or the higher soul."

- Master Choa Kok Sui in Meditations for Soul Realization

Quotations on the Inner Way according to Karlfried Graf Durckheim

"The fundamental prerequisites are: an inner need, right relation to the Inner Way, a persevering will, total participation, and the capacity for keeping silence and, above all, a turning to the Divine. Only when practice is completely imbued with and supported by the aspirant's submission to the Divine will the door open to those experiences of Being which will permit further progress on the Inner Way." -- Karlfried Graf Durckheim

"By leaving behind the "chest out-belly in" posture and attitude of the West and adopting the belly-centered posture and attitude of Hara, individuals can live a calm, grounded, and more balanced life."

NOTE by Ricardo B Serrano: With thanks and acknowledgement to the late Dr. Karlfried Graf Durckheim, PhD, a Western authority on Zen Buddhism, for his invaluable and essential guidance on spiritual awakening and healing through the fundamental spiritual principles and practices of his classic book on the Inner Way and Mastery -- "Hara: the Vital Center of Man."

"Man's "way inward" is the way of uniting himself with his Being wherein he partakes of Life beyond space and time. This is the way to maturity, the way that yields fruit in proportion to his success in integrating "himself" with his Self.

There is an inherent obstacle on the way inward which threatens even the sound healthy man, namely, that by the very structure of his consciousness, may assume complete control of the man's whole life. The door to the inner life can then re-open only when a man is able to break through the domination of the I and win contact with that Being and Life within him which evades all his "arrangements." But only an established inner

attitude enabling him constantly, from within this world, to participate in the Great Being will bring him the fruit of this integration. For only by his capacity to live and prove the Greater Life in the lesser one, only in the manifestation of Being in the world can man fulfill his appointed destiny as the simpler creatures do.

The way inwards rests on three factors. The first is an experience wherein the light of Being illuminates the darkness of life. The second is insight into the relationship of his worldly I and his transcendental Being, as well as into the difference between the state in which he is cut off from his Being and the right state which opens him to it. The third is practice, exercitium, which corrects the wrong working of the misguided I and builds up the right attitude in a right way. That is, a right attitude in which a man is permeable to the Greater Life which he embodies and by which he is enabled to perceive it in the world. He is then truly himself and the world of space and time becomes transparent for him in the Being which transcends space and time.

The way leading to this condition is by the transformation of the whole man, i.e., a unit of body, mind and soul. What keeps man estranged from Being consists not only in his being fettered by psychological complexes and by the rigidity of his thought-patterns, but also by the fact that they are fixed in his flesh and set fast in wrong bodily habits. So any renewal can be achieved only through the transformation of the whole man, and implies not only an intellectual and spiritual conversion, but also a transformation of the body and all its postures and movements. Without this bodily transformation all inner experience of Being comes to a standstill when the experience has passed, and the man inevitably falls victim again to his old, familiar fixing and classifying consciousness. Therefore practice must inevitably include practice of the body.

Just as the right inner state is clearly expressed in the symbolism of the harmoniously functioning body, so inner malformations appear as bodily malformations. These have one thing in common: lack of center. Lack of center implies either that a man is anchored too firmly in his upper body or that he lacks anchorage altogether. Only where a firm middle region exists is man's entire psycho-physical state properly entered.

The whole life attitude of a human being appears in his posture, in the relationship of tension and relaxation, and in breathing. Posture, tension and relaxation, and breath can never be exclusively physical factors. They are integral functions of the person manifesting himself analogously on the psychological and spiritual levels. For this reason it is possible to begin the work on the whole man with them."

"Becoming one with Being means transcending the structure patterns of ordinary consciousness. Therefore there can be no reanchoring in Being as long as experience, insight and practice do not break through the narrow circle of the usual rational consciousness pattern. All the struggling to acquire knowledge, all practice which merely strengthens the will, and all efforts to put feeling under discipline are doomed to failure when the Transcendental is the goal. A man has to overcome the dichotomy of objective and subjective consciousness, to let the original Unity penetrate his awareness and to let himself be embraced by it without wanting or trying to understand and hold it. When he admits the primal Unity which was within before and beyond all I-becoming he will find true renewal. By dropping his ego and submerging himself in the Primordial Life he will find Being within himself, become more and more at one with it, become through never flagging practice truly new, and as a renewed being prove himself as a witness of the Great Being."

"For the Westerner, also, if he progresses on the Inner Way, the world anchored in the I becomes a delusion. But it remains delusion for him only as long as his "I-reality" preserves its absolute character as the only reality. It ceases to be a delusion as soon as he is able to recognize it as the medium through which true Reality shows itself. Then the I-reality becomes transparent to Being and also the sphere of manifestation for him who bears within himself the One. The new man then constantly perceives the One in all colors, images, and patterns through which Being is refracted in the prism of the I. To realize Being in all and everything then becomes the sole function of his life. Time is no longer opposed to eternity but is the medium which reflects it. "Everything in space and time means ultimately only Eternity."

In this European or, more specifically, Christian view, a personal experiencing of the One is in fact only the beginning of the way of ultimate transformation. It is true that already in the never-ending discovery and rediscovery of that center of the primal Unity in man, new horizons open for the mind and new depths for the heart. But, when man lifts himself from the earth-center of his human nature to the heaven-center of his spirit and when, in his heart-center he joyously accepts the obligation to actualize the Original Unity and its inherent order within his existence in this world, then will his insight and practice flow out in one stream of true creative activity on earth. For the Kingdom of Heaven on earth is our true heritage and only within it will the real "circulation of light" be established."

Source: Hara: The Vital Center of Man by Karlfried Graf Durckheim, 2004

"Each of life's primal dilemmas is matched by its own saving power. Every recurrent anguish, longing, and hope finds its own special helper. The master is one of these helpers."

"Again and again, people driven by despair to seek the counsel and help demanded by their true nature, themselves construct the helpers they need, simply because they are suffering and searching so intensely. They receive a master's answer or a master's guidance from others who are by no means masters themselves."

"If we see Being as the one true reality and ourselves as the prisoners of the world, then the only way of fulfilling ourselves and getting back in touch with that ultimate reality is to leave the world utterly behind, die, and so finally enter the reality of All-One-Being. If, on the other hand, we see Life as transcending the antithesis of otherworldly Being and worldly reality, and manifestation of the Absolute in the worldly as our real objective, then we fulfill ourselves by witnessing to it in our ways of living, learning, and acting in the world."

Quotations on Inner Mastery
according to Karlfried Graf Durckheim

"Certainly a man who has devoted years or decades to the development of certain faculties can produce results which seem miraculous to the untrained. But the question is, what is the value of such achievements? If they are nothing but the result of a technique acquired from motives of pride they have no importance. Only when they give evidence of *inner mastery* are they of value." -- Karlfried Graf Durckheim

"One speaks of a "master" -- whether of an outer action or inner work -- only when success is achieved not only now and then, but with absolute certainty. Certainty of success presupposes more than perfected skill alone. What is this more? It is the state or condition of the performer which makes his performance infallible. However well-performed an action may be, however well-controlled a technique, as long as the man using it is subject to moods and atmosphere, unrelaxed and easily disturbed, for example, when he is being watched, then he is a master only in a very limited degree. He is master only of technique and not of himself. He controls the skill he has but not what he is in himself. And if a man can do more than he is his skill often fails him in critical moments. Real control over oneself can only be achieved by a special training, the outcome of which is not just technical skill, but an established frame of mind (Verfassung) which ensures the required result.

This is practice understood as exercise (exercitium). Its purpose is not an outer visible result but an inner achievement. In practice of this kind the person developing, not the deed or the visible work as such, is what matters. And as surely as genuine mastery of performance or skill presupposes a certain personal inner quality so, conversely, the preparing of oneself for performance or skill can be used as a way leading to inner mastery.

In this way the meaning of achieving outward and applied skill is transposed to the inner life. More important than outward success then is that personal quality which will, when developed produce not only the perfect external result, but which will have its real meaning and value within itself.

Understood thus, every art, every skill can become an opportunity to develop "on the Inner Way" and so a saying of the Japanese becomes understandable; "Archery and dancing, flower-arranging and singing, tea-drinking and wrestling -- it is all the same." From the viewpoint of performance of "work," this saying does not make sense, but once its underlying significance has been grasped -- man's true self-becoming -- then its meaning is clear.

For the Japanese every art as well as every sport has a purpose beyond mere outward achievement. In practicing it he aims at that quality of the whole man which produces results that appear to be casual, unintentional, without conscious effort -- just as an apple, when ripe, drops from the tree, without any help from the tree.

At the core of this attitude (Verfassung) is the imperturbability of the center of gravity in the true center which is Hara. I still remember my amazement when, in my early efforts to penetrate into the nature of the various Japanese "master practices" first in talks with masters of their arts, I heard again and again the word Hara pronounced with particular emphasis. Whether I talked to a master of swordsmanship, of dancing, of puppetry, of painting or of any other art, he invariably concluded his exposition of the relevant training by emphasizing Hara as the cardinal point of all effort. Thus I soon realized that this word obviously meant more than a mere prerequisite for the unfailing exercise of any technique. Hara seemed to be connected with something fundamental, something ultimate."

"In this way we can understand the words of an old Japanese whose opinion I asked concerning the miracles of the Indian Yogis. He said, "Certainly a man who has devoted years or decades to the development of certain faculties can produce results which seem miraculous to the untrained. But the question is, what is the value of such achievements? If they are nothing but the result of a technique acquired from motives of pride they have no importance. Only when they give evidence of inner mastery are they of value."

Such were the words of the old Japanese -- surprising words for us Europeans who idolize achievement for its own sake. In the East, what is considered masterly is only that which proves inner maturity, which produces ripe fruit as a tree does effortlessly."

"To summarize: anchorage in the vital center which is Hara guarantees man enjoyment of a power which enables him to master life in a new and different way. It is a mysteriously sustaining, ever renewing, ordering and forming power, as well as a liberating and integrating one.

As a spiritual being man seeks something beyond and above secure existence. He seeks completeness within himself and in the world. He is in search of an accomplished form that will perfectly actualize the inner meaning residing in it. Both in recognition and in action he is serving the "objective," the idea latent in a thing, a work accomplished. He feels himself obligated by inherent laws and in addition he seeks his fellow man for what he is. He perceives him in his unique being.

Significant and effective accomplishment of any given objective is hindered by the pre-existence of firmly fixed ideas and concepts, and fixation within the ego results in an ineradicable entanglement within the sphere of the personal -- all-too-personal.

Effective recognition, action, and creation pre-supposes a detachment which will enable a man to perceive the "other" in the other's own nature and at his own value. Only real detachment from an ego clinging to its position, and freedom from fixed pre-judgements makes possible an elasticity of functioning which is indispensable for the accomplishment of any objective undertaking.

All ability is blocked when a person is bound within his little I, when he faces his tasks with and from the wrong center of gravity. For then he is either fixed or trapped. If he is able to free himself from the yoke of the ego and to place himself in the right center he soon gains not only a correct perspective but he can also make the best use of his knowledge. Thus precision of functioning pre-supposes that flexibility-in-depth which is tantamount to the ego's ability to release its grip on the steering wheel to which it clings so tenaciously.

The highest kind of skill is shown in the long run by a "letting-it-happen," which implies abandoning the already achieved, but it is blocked when each repetition calls for a conscious act of will. Such abandoning is synonymous with the letting go of the "doing" I. When it no longer interferes, when ambition and self-seeking are absent and the necessary effort is unforced, skill and ability come into full play. For then a man allows his ability, freed of all personal factors, of all fixations, to be used as an instrument in the service of the deeper power which will do the work for him. For this power to take effect there must be an anchorage in Hara, where there is no ego.

Any clinging to the ego position is also a cause of intellectual poverty. It actually blinds a man to the new perspectives which open out at every step of advancing perception or understanding. It impedes the creative powers of the mind. But the man whose ego is continually held in check is constantly discovering new possibilities.

Hara liberates the creative imagination. One who is freed from the ego becomes aware of new images arising from deeper levels. This is proved by the inexhaustible wealth of imagery arising in dreams. The tissue of established concepts and images hampering the imagination becomes penetrable, whether in sleeping or in waking, only in the degree to which the ego withdraws and to which the individual in his waking state finds his center of gravity elsewhere.

Thus in the mental realm, achieving Hara means the release of powers latent in the depths that endow man in all his activities with creative energy and a sense of actuality. Freed from the bondage of established patterns of the past, he is creatively united with the task in hand."

Source: Hara: The Vital Center of Man by Karlfried Graf Durckheim, 2004

Quotations from the Power of Now & A New Earth by Eckhart Tolle

"Nature is a portal to presence." – Eckhart Tolle

"The spiritual teachings of Eckhart Tolle have greatly resonated with the stillness of my inner Self and enlightenment -- awareness of Being and Qigong state of Self-realization -- that I highly recommend his books "The Power of Now" and "A New Earth" to every seeker on the Path as indispensable guideposts to spiritual enlightenment." -- Qigong Master Ricardo B Serrano

"True love is the recognition of the formless in the other.

You are the light in which these forms appear.

You are the sky. The clouds are what happens, what comes and goes.

Seek out a tree, and let it teach you stillness.

If your mind is still, you can sense the peace that emanates from the earth.

We're here to find that dimension within ourselves that is deeper than thought.

Form and space interpenetrate each other, without as well as within.

Outer space and inner space are ultimately one." -- Stillness Amidst The World

Powerful Quotes from The Power of Now
by Eckhart Tolle

Having access to that formless realm is truly liberating. It frees you from bondage to form and identification with form. It is life in its undifferentiated state prior to its fragmentation into multiplicity. We may call it the Unmanifested, the invisible Source of all things, the Being within all beings. It is a realm of deep stillness and peace, but also of joy and intense aliveness. Whenever you are present, you become "transparent" to some extent to the light, the pure consciousness that emanates from this Source. You also realize that the light is not separate from who you are but constitutes your very essence.

Identification with your mind creates an opaque screen of concepts, labels, images, words, judgments, and definitions that blocks all true relationship. It comes between you and yourself, between you and your fellow man and woman, between you and nature, between you and God. It is this screen of thought that creates the illusion of separateness, the illusion that there is you and a totally separate "other." You then forget the essential fact that, underneath the level of physical appearances and separate forms, you are one with all that is.

Being is not only beyond but also deep within every form as its innermost invisible and indestructible essence. This means that it is accessible to you now as your own deepest self, your true nature. But don't seek to grasp it with your mind. Don't try to understand it. You can know it only when the mind is still. When you are present, when your attention is fully and intensely in the Now, Being can be felt, but it can never be understood mentally. To regain awareness of Being and to abide in that state of "feeling-realization" is enlightenment.

Be present as the watcher of your mind -- of your thoughts and emotions as well as your reactions in various situations. Be at least as interested in your reactions as in the situation or person that causes you to react. Notice also how often your attention is in the past or future. Don't judge or analyze what you observe. Watch the thought, feel the emotion, observe the reaction. Don't make a personal problem out of them. You will then feel something more powerful than any of those things that you observe: the still, observing presence itself behind the content of your mind, the silent watcher.

You are not just a meaningless fragment in an alien universe, briefly suspended between life and death, allowed a few short-lived pleasures followed by pain and ultimate annihilation. Underneath your outer form, you are connected with something so vast, so immeasurable and sacred, that it cannot be spoken of -- yet I am speaking of it now. I am speaking of it now not to give you something to believe in but to show you how you can know it for yourself.

The word enlightenment conjures up the idea of some superhuman accomplishment, and the ego likes to keep it that way, but it is simply your natural state of felt oneness with Being. It is a state of connectedness with something immeasurable and indestructible, something that, almost paradoxically, is essentially you and yet is much greater than you. It is finding your true nature beyond name and form.

Beyond the beauty of external forms, there is more here: something that cannot be named, something ineffable, some deep, inner, holy essence. Whenever and wherever there is beauty, this inner essence shines through somehow. It only reveals itself to you when you are present.

Many expressions that are in common usage, and sometimes the structure of language itself, reveal the fact that people don't know who they are. You say: "He lost his life" or "my life," as if life were something that you can possess or lose. The truth is: you don't have a life, you are life. The One Life, the one consciousness that pervades the entire universe and takes temporary form to experience itself as a stone or blade of grass, as an animal, a person, a star or a galaxy.

Can you sense deep within that you already know that? Can you sense that you already are That?

Powerful Quotes from A New Earth
by Eckhart Tolle

"Your inner purpose is to awaken. It is as simple as that. You share that purpose with every other person on the planet -- because it is the purpose of humanity. Your inner purpose is an essential part of the purpose of the whole, the universe and its emerging intelligence. Your outer purpose can change over time. It varies greatly from person to person. Finding and living in alignment with the inner purpose is the foundation for fulfilling your outer purpose. It is the basis for true success. Without alignment, you can still achieve certain things through effort, struggle, determination, and sheer hard work or cunning. But there is no joy in such endeavor, and it invariably ends in some form of suffering."

"Awareness is the power that is concealed within the present moment. This is why we may also call it Presence.

The ultimate purpose of human existence, which is to say, your purpose, is to bring that power into this world.

Your primary purpose is to enable consciousness to flow into what you do. The secondary purpose is whatever you want to achieve through the doing. Whereas the notion of purpose before was always associated with future, there is now a deeper purpose that can only be found in the present, through denial of time."

"Only by awakening can you know the true meaning of that word.

Instead of being lost in your thinking, when you awaken you recognize yourself as the awareness behind it. Thinking then ceases to be a self-serving autonomous activity that takes possession of you and runs your life. Awareness takes over from thinking. Instead of being in charge of your life, thinking becomes the servant of awareness. Awareness is conscious connection with universal intelligence. Another word for it is Presence: consciousness without thought.

What is the relationship between awareness and thinking? Awareness is the space in which thoughts exist when that space has become conscious of itself."

Quotations from the Ancient Siddha Lineage Tradition and Sri Vidya Upasana

"One's own thoughts is one's world. What a person thinks is what he becomes - that is the eternal mystery. If the mind dwells within the supreme Self, One enjoys undying happiness." -- Maitri Upanishad

The following quotations from the ancient Shaivite and Vedic scriptures are based on the ancient true path of the Siddha (enlightened liberated yogi) lineage and philosophy of Kashmir Shaivism and Vedanta that, I personally believe, has close similarity with the Taoist and Buddhist tantric philosophy and psychology of liberation. Kashmir Shaivism is a nondual philosophy that recognizes the entire universe as a manifestation of Shiva, as the play of His divine conscious energy, Shakti, or Chiti. In Shaivism, Supreme Shiva (Paramashiva) is the all-pervasive supreme Reality, the unmoving, transcendent divine Consciousness. In the Hindu trinity, Shiva, or the Self, is the aspect of God as the destroyer of ignorance.

May the following quotations from the ancient Shaivite and Vedic scriptures lead you to further additional Kundalini Shakti (Qi) exploration, study, chanting, mantra-repetition, selfless service, satsang, spending time in the company of saints and practice of the Guru principle and their basic centering meditation techniques to purify the mind and break the chain of inner words that will eventually assist you in your spiritual journey and liberation, as the practices have assisted me greatly as a long-time Yoga and Qigong practitioner, toward love, transformation, spontaneous healing and personal freedom through Self-realization or Realization of Buddha nature. Siddha Guru Baba Muktananda writes, "The universe is a garden for us to roam with love. It is not intended as a source of attachment, jealousy, hatred, or anxiety. These only destroy our equanimity. Give up all desires. If something comes, let it come; if something goes, let it go. It is all Shiva's play. This is not a mere universe; it is the image of Him. Knowing it as Shiva, love it. Meditate on the awareness that all conscious beings as well as inert matter are Shiva. Having the knowledge of Shiva, understand that the world is the embodiment of Him."

"It is to attain the bliss of samadhi that we should meditate, that we should have our Kundalini awakened by the grace of a master. We do not meditate to attain God, because we have already attained Him. We meditate so that we can become aware of God manifest within us."

And this is why he always tells everyone, "Meditate on your Self, honor your Self, understand your Self, worship your Self, for God dwells within you as you."

"Ignorance is the root cause of all suffering. It is also the forgetfulness of one's own Self." - Shankaracharya, Aparokshanubhuti, 17

Lokananda samadhi sukham - "The bliss of the world is the ecstasy of samadhi." - Shiva Sutras, I, 18
"Moksa or liberation is nothing else but the awareness of one's true nature." - Abhinavagupta, Tantra I, p. 192

"Neither reject anything, nor accept, abide in your essential Self which is an Eternal presence." Abhinavagupta, Anuttarastika, 2

"Why do you look for Him only in churches or mosques? Do you not see His creation? Where does He not abide? The whole universe made by Him recites His tale." – Sarmad

"He is the real Guru Who can reveal the form of the formless before your eyes; who teaches the simple path, without rites or ceremonies; Who does not make you close your doors, and hold your breath, and renounce the world; Who makes you perceive the Supreme Spirit whenever the mind attaches itself; Who teaches you to be still in the midst of all your activities. Fearless, always immersed in bliss, he keeps the spirit of yoga in the midst of enjoyments." - Kabir

"Like oil in sesame seeds, butter in cream, water in the river bed, fire in tinder, the Self dwells within. Realize that Self through meditation." - Shvetashvatara Upanishad

"Just by repeating the Name, that which cannot be understood will be understood. Just by repeating the Name, that which cannot be seen will be seen." - Jnaneshwar Maharaj

"Contemplate Kundalini, Who is supreme Consciousness, who plays from the base of the spine to the crown of the head, Who shines like a flash of lightning, Who is fine as the fiber of the lotus stalk, Who has the brilliant radiance of countless suns, Who is a shaft of light as cool as hundreds of nectarian moonbeams." - Shri Vidya Antar Yaga

"One's own thoughts is one's world. What a person thinks is what he becomes - that is the eternal mystery. If the mind dwells within the supreme Self, One enjoys undying happiness."
- Maitri Upanishad

"Yoga is the stilling of the vrittis [modifications] of the mind." - Patanjali Yoga Sutras, I, 2

"Smaller than the smallest, greater than the greatest. This Self forever dwells in the hearts of all. A person freed from desire, with mind and senses purified, Beholds the glory of the Self and is without sorrows." - Katha Upanishad

"He who continually perceives this entire universe as a sport of the universal Consciousness is truly Self-realized beyond any doubt; he is liberated in this body." - Vasuguptacharya, Spanda Shastra

"There is neither bondage nor liberation for me. Bondage and liberation frighten only those who are ignorant of their essential nature. The universe appears as a reflection in the intellect like the image of the sun in water." - Vijnana Bhairava, 135

"O my blessed beloved, awake! Why do you sleep in ignorance." – Kabir

Baba Muktananda says, "Chanting the divine name is the most sublime way to develop inner love. The divine lover pursues God through his divine name."

"Chant the mantra with great feeling. Chant with all your heart and the bliss will come. No negativities can withstand the bliss of the Lord's name."

"The dancer in this field of universal dance is his Self of universal consciousness." - Shiva Sutra 3.9
What is this universal dance? It is everything that you experience in your life. It may be coming. It may be going. It may be birth, death, joy, sadness, depression, happiness, enjoyment. All of this forms part of the universal dance, and this dance is a drama. In this field of drama, the actor is your own nature, your own Self of universal consciousness. This Self of universal consciousness is the one who is aware, he is the actor in this universal drama. Those who are not aware are not actors, they are played in this drama. They experience sadness, they experience enjoyment, they become joyful, they become depressed. But those who are aware, they are always elevated; they are the real players in this drama.

So it is your own Self of universal consciousness which is, in fact, the actor. Why? Because he acts. The actor is he who conceals his real nature. When you conceal the real nature of your being and, to the public, reveal another form of your being, that is the behavior of acting. Because when any person, say, a person named Denise, is the real actor and, as an actor, she appears as Lord Krisna, as Lord Siva, as a woman, as a child, as a silly fellow, then the real and actual state of her being is concealed. So for others, the actual state of her being is concealed and a superficial formation is revealed. But for her, the actual state of her being is not concealed. She knows she is Denise. At the time of becoming Lord Krishna or Siva or Jesus Christ, she is aware of her being Denise. In herself, she knows she is really Denise.

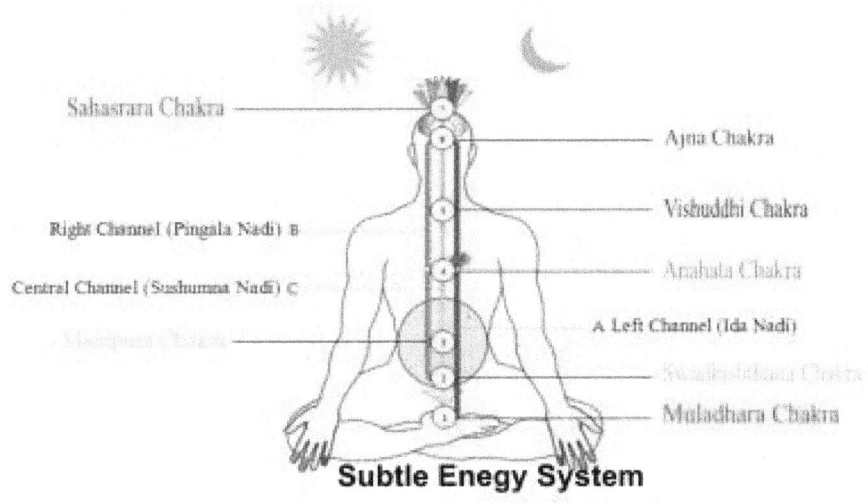

Shiva and Shakti reunited via Vagus Nerve Qi-healing
by Acharya Ricardo B Serrano
http://freedomhealthrecovery.com/blog/?p=14147

Hreem Shreem Sauh Hasakaphrem

"Nothing has the greatest power to heal, but Self". The body has the innate power to heal itself, we just need to allow and open up.

To be grounded in the Self, to be at home with the Self, to be established in the Self, then the wisdom of the body awakens and guides you. That is the yogic concept of healing.

When Shiva and Shakti are reunited, samadhi is the outcome.

When the ida and pingala pathways are rebalanced and reunited, and the kundalini shakti in the sushumna (middle channel) is awakened via the vagus nerve Qi-healing with Sri Vidya chanting (of mantras), samadhi and healing are the outcome. See Subtle Energy Sytem, page 57

Thus, it is said in kundalini yoga that when Shiva and Shakti are reunited, samadhi is the resultant outcome. See Subtle Energy System, *Return to Oneness with Shiva*, page 133

The ida and pingala pathways correspond to the vagus nerve that runs in the left and right side of the neck that connect to the points in the organs down to the abdomen.

The vagus nerve also corresponds to the thrusting channels of the eight extraordinary meridians which can be stimulated by the eight extraordinary meridians Qigong and intranasal light therapy. See 8 extraordinary meridians Qigong, *Oneness with Shiva*, page 65

– Ricardo B Serrano, R.Ac., Originator of Vagus Nerve Qi-healing

– Excerpts from page 149, Return to Oneness with Shiva

– See Kundalini Shakti, page 21; Intranasal Light Therapy, page 94; Sri Yantra, page 119; Read Why the health care system is broken, page 138 and *The Cure & Cause of Cancer*

Reasons to Address Your Stress

"It's not stress that kills us, it is our reaction to it." -- Hans Seyle

The stress hormones that trigger the fight-or-flight reaction caused by persistent stress over the long term pose serious threats to your health which is why you must address your stress.

Elevated levels of stress hormone cortisol lead to inflammatory conditions such as atherosclerosis. Cortisol suppresses the immune system and also lead to flare-ups of existing conditions such as ulcers, asthma, cold sores or eczema. Elevated levels of stress hormone adrenaline elevate both blood pressure and heart rate increasing your risk of heart attack or stroke.

The chemical changes created by stress can alter brain function and trigger anxiety and depression that produce chronic insomnia, obesity and substance abuse; affects cognitive function such as short and long term memory; and reduces sex drive leading to impotence and lower fertility.

Symptoms of persistent stress include anxious or negative thoughts or feelings, loss of concentration, frequent illness, changes in diet or sleep patterns, nervousness, chest pain, irritability, procrastination, and feelings of isolation.

While stress produces many negative effects, they are reversible. In fact, stress can be managed and reduced by going with and being in the flow of all things using Omkabah Lightbody Activation, breathing, meditation, Qigong and other natural Oriental healing modalities to cultivate the Three Treasures Jing, Qi and Shen.

According to Qi Dao Master Lama Tantrapa, "Struggling against the flow of a night- dream is a sure way to turn it into a nightmare. Similarly, if you struggle against the flow of your daily life, you single-handedly turn your life into a nightmare. Going against the flow of things only exhausts your energy, takes a toll on your health, and wastes your time. As soon as you realize that life's challenges can be perceived as learning opportunities rather than problems, you will become less tense or "stressed-out" and find yourself in the flow of life. Being in the flow will empower you to live your dreams."

Our lives are filled with stress reflected by our mental attitude and emotional experience. Because of our own ignorance, we look for love, happiness, peace, joy and contentment outside where they are not. Shaktipat meditation is a simple and direct means to experience within you an ocean of love, peace, joy, happiness and well-being in a continuous basis.

"One's own thought is one's world. What a person thinks is what he becomes -- That is the eternal mystery. If the mind dwells within the supreme Self, One enjoys undying happiness." - Maitri Upanishad

According to Siddha Guru Baba Muktananda, "There is one great obstacle that keeps us from knowing the Self, and that is the mind. The mind veils the inner Self and hides it from us. It makes us feel that God is far away and that happiness must be found outside. Yet the same mind that separates us from the Self also helps us to reunite with it. That is why the ancient sages, who were true psychologists, concluded that the mind is the source of both bondage and liberation, the source of both sorrow and joy, our worst enemy as well as our greatest friend. That is why, if there is anything worth knowing in this world, it is the mind.

The sages of the Upanishads said that the mind is the body of the Self (Consciousness). The Self shines through the mind and makes it function. But although the Self is so close to the mind, the mind does not know it. The mind is always moving outside, focusing on external objects, and as a result it has become very dull. It has lost the capacity to reflect the radiance of the Self, just as a lake whose waters are filled with silt loses its capacity to reflect the sun. However, when we practice meditation, the mind goes deeper and deeper within, and becomes more and more quiet. When it is truly still, we begin to drink the nectar of the Self. That is why yoga and meditation came into existence: to quiet the mind, to make it free of thoughts, and to enable it to touch its own source...

True psychology is born of meditation. The scriptures of meditation are the greatest works of psychology. Psychology is not just talking, talking, talking. Real psychology is yoga. There was a great sage called Maharshi Patanjali whose Yoga Sutras are the authoritative text on yoga. Patanjali said that through yoga one can still the movements of the mind. That is true psychology. One cannot cure the troubles of the mind by talking, nor can one steady the mind by using herbs or drugs. Drugs may calm the mind for a while, but once the effect of the drugs fade away, the mind will return to its former state. One can straighten out the mind only by making it still, by calming the thoughts and feelings that cause it to become agitated. If psychotherapists truly understood what the mind is and improved their own minds with meditation, they would be able to practice great therapy...

In our yoga scriptures, the mind is represented as the horse that pulls a chariot. The reins are in your hands. If you let the horse go where it wishes, it will take you into a pit. You should not be defeated by your own mind. You should still the mind, purify the mind, discipline the mind. You should bring it under control with your intellect..." See Vagus Nerve Qi-healing, page 58

Qi-healing COVID-19 naturally

I would like to share with you how to prevent and recover from COVID-19 by boosting the immune system naturally with safe effective therapies that work for me and others despite what drug dependents say.

As a form of Qi-healing, I personally use Vielight 655 Prime daily as an adjunct to Qigong with herbs to maintain my immune system health. I also use Vielight 810 Neuro Gamma every two days to enhance my brain function. – Ricardo B Serrano, R.Ac.

Vielight 655 Prime strengthens the immune system which can be a strong deterrent to coronavirus (nCoV) infection. – Ricardo B Serrano, R.Ac.

Coconut oil with 655 Prime intranasal light therapy (blood oxygenation) and Eight extraordinary meridians Qigong are the best immune system boosters to ward off viruses in my international travels. – Ricardo B Serrano, R.Ac.

Up-regulation of cytochrome c oxidase (CCO) by intranasal light therapy (ILT) can optimize the oxygenation of the blood of ill patients with COVID-19 whose lungs are affected reducing the oxygenation of their blood. ILT also triggers the release of nitric oxide (NO) that inhibits the replication cycle of Severe Acute Respiratory Syndrome Coronavirus. See Intranasal Light Therapy, page 94

"Coconut oil, CBD oil, intranasal light therapy and Qigong are the best immune system boosters to ward off COVID-19." – Ricardo B Serrano, R.Ac.

Can CBD help with Coronavirus Cytokine Storm? In inflammatory states (such as coronavirus cytokine storm), CBD (Cannabidiol) in the form of CBD oil can calm inflammation. Moreover, CBD, but not THC, up-regulates the activation of the STAT3 transcription factor, an element of homeostatic mechanism(s) inducing anti-inflammatory events. For more info, read *The Cure & Cause of Cancer*

DISCLAIMER: The above statements are not my claims but claims by Vielight.com and my other teachers.

The Three Treasures Jing, Qi and Shen according to Ron Teeguarden

"All disease and suffering arise out of the imbalances of the Three Treasures, Jing, Qi and Shen." -- Ron Teeguarden, M.H.

NOTE by Ricardo B Serrano, Master Herbalist: With thanks and acknowledgement to Dan-O Sun Sha Ron Teeguarden, Master Herbalist, whose knowledge on the Three Treasures, Chinese tonic herbs and Korean Mountain Taoism have assisted Oriental medicine practitioners including myself in my quest toward radiant health and happiness through his classic book, The Ancient Wisdom of Chinese Tonic Herbs, and herbal teachings at Ron Teeguarden's Blog World.

In the Daoist tradition, which forms the foundation of the traditional Oriental healing and health-promoting arts, there are said to be Three Treasures that in effect constitute our life. These are known as Jing, Qi and Shen. There are no exact translations for these terms in English, but they are generally translated as Essence, Vitality, and Spirit.

The ultimate goal of all of the Oriental healing and health-promoting arts is to cultivate, balance and expand the Three Treasures. At the highest level of the Oriental healing arts, the practitioner is attempting to harmonize all aspects of one's being. This is accomplished by focusing one's attention on the Three Treasures.

The author's great teacher, Master Sung Jin Park, used to describe the Three Treasures by comparing them to a burning candle. Jing is like the wax and wick, which are the substantial parts of the candle. They are made of material, which is essentially condensed energy. The flame of the lit candle is likened to Qi, for this is the energetic activity of the candle, which eventually results in the burning out of the candle. The radiance given off by the flaming candle is Shen. The larger the candle and the better the quality of the wax and wick, the steadier will be its flame and the longer the candle will last. The greater and steadier the flame, the steadier the light given off and the greater the light. Master Park described the Three Treasures in some detail:

There are three treasures in the human body. These are known as Jing, Qi and Shen. Of these three, only Qi has received some recognition in the West so far. Qi is but one of the Three Treasures -- the other two are equally wondrous.

Jing has been called the "superior ultimate" treasure, even though even in a healthy, radiant body, the quantity is small. Jing existed before the body existed, and this Jing enters the body tissues and becomes the root of our body. When we keep Jing within our body, our body can be vigorous. If a person cares for the Cavity of Jing [a space within the lower abdomen], and does not hurt it recklessly, it is very easy to enjoy a life of great longevity. Without Jing energy, we cannot live.

Qi is the invisible life force which enables the body to think and perform voluntary movement. The power of Qi can be seen in the power that enables a person to move and live. It can be seen in the movement of energy in the cosmos and in all other movements and changes. Coming from heaven into the body through the nose (Yang Gate), it circulates through the twelve meridians [the energy circuitry of the body] to nourish and preserve the inner organs.

Shen energy is similar to the English meaning of the words "mind" and "spirit." It is developed by the combination of Jing and Qi energy. When these two treasures are in balance, the mind is strong, the spirit is great, the emotions are under control, and the body is strong and healthy. But it is very difficult to expect a sound mind to be cultivated without sound Jing and Qi. An old proverb says that a sound mind lives in a sound body. When cultivated, Shen will bring peace of mind.

When we develop Jing, we get a large amount of Qi automatically. When we have a large amount of Qi, we will also have strong Shen, and we will become bright and glowing as a holy man.

Jing (Essence)

Jing is the first Treasure and is translated as "Regenerative Essence," or simply as "Essence." Jing is the refined energy of the body. It provides the foundation for all activity and is said to be the "root" of our vitality. Jing is the primal energy of life. It is closely associated with our genetic potential, and is associated with the aging process. Jing is stored energy and provides the reserves required to adapt to all the various stresses encountered in life. Since Jing is concentrated energy, it manifests materially. Jing also is said to control a number of primary human functions: the reproductive organs and their various substances and functions; the power and clarity of the mind; and the integrity of one's physical structure. Jing, which is a blend of Yin and Yang energy, is said to be stored in the "Kidney." Jing is generally associated these days with the hormones of the reproductive and adrenal glands, and Jing is the vital essence concentrated in the sperm and ova.

It is considered extremely difficult to enhance the original Jing after conception, although it is not at all difficult to deplete and weaken it, and thus to weaken and shorten one's life. The only way to strengthen the original Jing is through specific highly sophisticated yogic techniques such as those developed by the Daoists and by consuming certain potent tonic herbs known as Jing tonics. The purpose of taking Jing tonic herbs is to maintain healthy levels of postnatal Jing. If postnatal Jing is maintained at sufficient levels, prenatal Jing is used much more slowly and the aging process is slowed down.

When Jing is strong, vitality and youthfulness remain. Strong Jing energy in the Kidneys, so the Chinese say, will lead to a long and vigorous life, while a loss of Jing will result in physical and mental degeneration and a shortening of one's life. Jing is essential to life and when it runs low our life force is severely diminished and thus we lose all power to adapt. The quantity of Essence determines both our life span and the ultimate vitality of our life. Jing is burned up in the body by life itself, but most especially by chronic and acute stress and excessive behavior, including overwork, excessive emotionalism, substance abuse, chronic pain or illness, and marital excess (especially in men). Excessive menstrual patterns, pregnancy and childbirth can result in a dramatic drain on the Jing of a woman, especially in middle aged women. When Jing is depleted below a level required to survive, we die. Eventually everyone runs out of Jing and thus everyone dies (at least physically).

Qi (Vitality)

Qi, the second Treasure, is the energy that creates our vitality. Through the constant interaction of Yin and Yang change is brought into being. Qi is the activity of Yin and Yang. Movement, functioning and thought is the result of Qi. The nature of Qi is to move. In the Three Treasures system includes both Energy and Blood. It nourishes and protects us. Qi is said to be produced as a result of the functions of the Lungs and Spleen. Therefore, Qi tonics strengthen the digestive, assimilative and respiratory functions.

When Qi condenses, it becomes Jing. Fast moving Qi is considered to be Yang while slow moving Qi is Yin. In the system of the Three Treasures, blood is considered to be a part of the Qi component of our being. Blood is said to be produced from the food ingested after the Qi has been extracted through the action of the Spleen. The red blood cells are said to be nutritive and are thus associated with the Ying Qi (Yin), while the white blood cells are protective and are associated with Wei Qi (Yang). Qi tonics are generally believed to have potent immune modulating activity. Qi tonics, composed of Energy and/or Blood tonics, increase our ability to function fully and adaptively as human beings.

Shen (Spirit)

Shen is the third Treasure. Shen is the Holy Spirit which directs Qi. It may also be translated as our "higher consciousness." This is ultimately the most important of the Three Treasures because it reflects our higher nature as human beings. Chinese masters say that Shen is the all-embracing love that resides in our "Heart," a primary organ system. Shen is the spiritual radiance of a human being and is the ultimate and most refined level of energetics in the universe. Shen is not considered to be an emotion, or even a state of mind. It presides over the emotions and manifests as all-encompassing compassion, and non-discriminating, non-judgemental awareness. Shen is expressed as love, compassion, kindness, generosity, acceptance, forgiveness and tolerance. It manifests as our wisdom and our ability to see all sides of all issues, our ability to rise above the world of right and wrong, good and bad, yours and mine, high and low, and so on. Shen is our higher knowledge that everything is one, even though nature manifests dualistically and cyclically, often obscuring our vision and creating illusion.

Our true Spirit, which the Chinese call Shen, is the spark of divinity that resides within the heart of every human being and manifests as love, kindness, compassion, generosity, giving, tolerance, forgiveness, mercy, tenderness and the appreciation of beauty. It is the Spirit of a human being as the divine messenger, the channel of God's will and love. Shen is the purpose of all spiritual paths. It is the Buddha's desire to end suffering and it is Christ's love and compassion... Shen manifests only when the heart is open. Once the heart is open, Shen manifests as light that illuminates the path of a man or woman in life's journey toward the spiritual goal and along the spiritual path.

Excerpted from The Ancient Wisdom of Chinese Tonic Herbs

How to Achieve Stillness

How do you achieve stillness? You do not achieve stillness by stopping the thinking process, but by being aware of the inner stillness. Where is this inner stillness located? It is in the "gap". The mantra OM helps, but it is not enough. What is more important is being aware of the interval between two OMs. Between two OMs, there is a gap or stillness. This is called Meditation on the Gap.

When you do Awareness Meditation on the Breath, you must not only be aware of the inhalation and exhalation. What is more important is that one should be aware of the gap between inhalations and exhalations, and between exhalations and inhalations. Within this gap there is stillness. One must be aware repeatedly of this stillness.

Practicing Awareness Meditation on the Thoughts is advisable. Not only should you be aware of the thoughts going in and out of the mind, but also be aware of the interval between the two thoughts, because in this interval there is stillness. By repeatedly being aware of this inner stillness, one will be able to achieve expansion of consciousness.

The practice of repeating mantras is also good, but like other meditational practices it is more important to be aware of the gap between the two mantras because the stillness is in the gap.

Psalm 46:10 states, "Be still and know that I am God." By practicing stillness, one becomes aware of the Divine Presence not only within one's self; one also becomes aware of the pervasive presence of the Divine."

Excerpted from Master Choa Kok Sui's Meditations for Soul Realization, 2000.

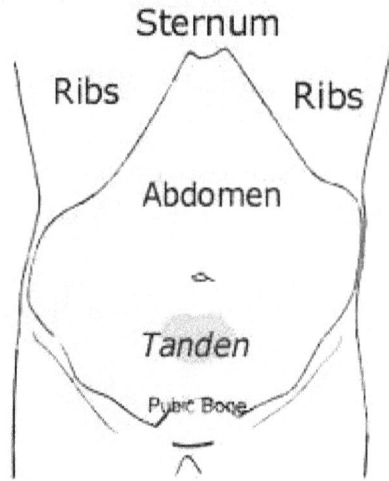

Cultivating Qi in the Hara & Its Energetic Pathways

"I heard ancient people were able to live to one hundred years and still be the same as when young. But nowadays, when fifty years old our activities decrease. How is this? Is it due to the times, or have humans lost something?" the Yellow Emperor asked.

"The ancient people knew the way, the Tao, and the rule of Yin <-> Yang and could get harmony of the numbers. The ancient people could control their eating habits. They knew the rules of life, waking and sitting. They don't overwork. For these reasons, they were healthy and balanced in body and mind and were able to live one hundred years. But today, people are not like this, they drink too much alcohol and think about sex and after drinking will go to bed and lose their Jing according to their sexual desire. At the same time as losing their Jing, they lose and disperse the truth. They don't know how to keep the body healthy. They don't know how to control their mind and cannot control their desires. They are against the living pleasure, the Tao." the physician Chi Po answered.

From the Huang Ti Nei Ching, Su Wen, Chapter One.

"The four seasons and Yin and Yang are the beginning and ending of everything, the root of birth and death. If ones goes against the rule of this one can get injury, creating general catastrophies, like a flood, which affect all others as well. If one doesn't go against the rule disease doesn't occur, this is the Tao."
From the Huang Ti Nei Ching, Su Wen, Chapter Two

The following excerpts from the book Five Elements & Ten Stems supported by the classics Nan Ching, Ling Shu and Huang Jing Ching show the importance in cultivating Qi energy in the Hara and its energetic pathways through Qigong, meditation, herbs, diet, exercise, acupressure, and acupuncture for stress management, holistic health and well-being:

The energies of the Heaven <-> Man <-> Earth continuum are assimilated and drawn into the Hara. Located in the abdomen, the center of the body, the Hara is the central point for all of these energies. The Hara is described as the realm of the "Moving Chi between the Kidneys" and is centered around the "Sea of Chi," Chi Hai or Tanden and the umbilicus. This understanding is found in some of the earliest texts. In the Huang Jing Ching, or "Yellow Jing Textbook," the following description is given.

"The Yin Chi and Yang Chi meet and cross together {as in sex} and then Jing comes down and Jing alchemically transforms to Shen. Jing and Shen combine together to take on some form, and then come up to the Nine heavens to become the Chi of the Nine Heavens. The Chi coming down to Chi Hai meets Shen and then the person is created." But today, people are not like this, they drink too much alcohol and think about sex and after drinking will go to bed and lose their Jing according to their sexual desire. At the same time as losing their Jing, they lose and disperse the truth. They don't know how to keep the body healthy. They don't know how to control their mind and cannot control their desires. They are against the living pleasure, the Tao." the physician Chi Po answered.

The Nan Ching specifies the source of Chi as the Hara and the Breath. The Ling Shu ties both the Breath of Heaven and the Chi of food and water to formation of the true Chi. This quote from the Nan Ching tells us that the "source of vital Chi" is the Hara:

"The Hara ... the source of vital Chi..... is the gate of breathing."

Wang Shu He, who wrote a little known but brilliant treatise on the Nan Ching, explicitly states when commenting on this section of the Nan Ching that air when drawn into the abdomen creates Chi:

"Breath {gas/air from breathing} reaches to the inside {of the abdomen}. The Chi grows and then becomes solid; this protects against evil injuring the body. Protecting on the inside and defending on the outside, this is Chi."

This passage is very similar to the preceding quotation from San Dai Ji Jin Wen Tsun. Both emphasize the distention of the abdomen as air is drawn in from proper breathing. it would follow that the solidity mentioned by each is the elastic flexibility of a healthy Hara.

According to information from the Ling Shu, the energies of Heaven <-> Man <-> Earth interact to form the True Chi. One aspect or equivalent of True Chi is the Source Chi. It is in the Hara, the area of "the Moving Chi between the Kidneys," that all energies interact to create the basic or Source Chi of the body:

"True Chi is the prenatal Chi from the parents, Chi of the breathing from Heaven and Chi of food and water from Earth, mixing together."

The idea of energies coming down to the Hara or Chi Hai (Tanden) pervades the classic references. The Hara was seen as the merging point of the various energies and the source of True Chi. One aspect of this Chi forms, creates, or becomes the Five Elements energies. More precisely, this aspect of the energies presents, creates, or becomes the Ten Stems energies which are described by the Five Elements system. A second or additional aspect of this Basic or Source Chi forms, creates, becomes or nourishes the twelve meridians (The Twelve Branches).

The energetic anatomy is clear. The Hara is the center, the ultimate source of Chi. The Triple Warmer is the energetic connection of the Hara to the Source points of all the meridians. It is the "root" of health and life. Before any other treatment is administered, we need to treat the condition of the Hara.

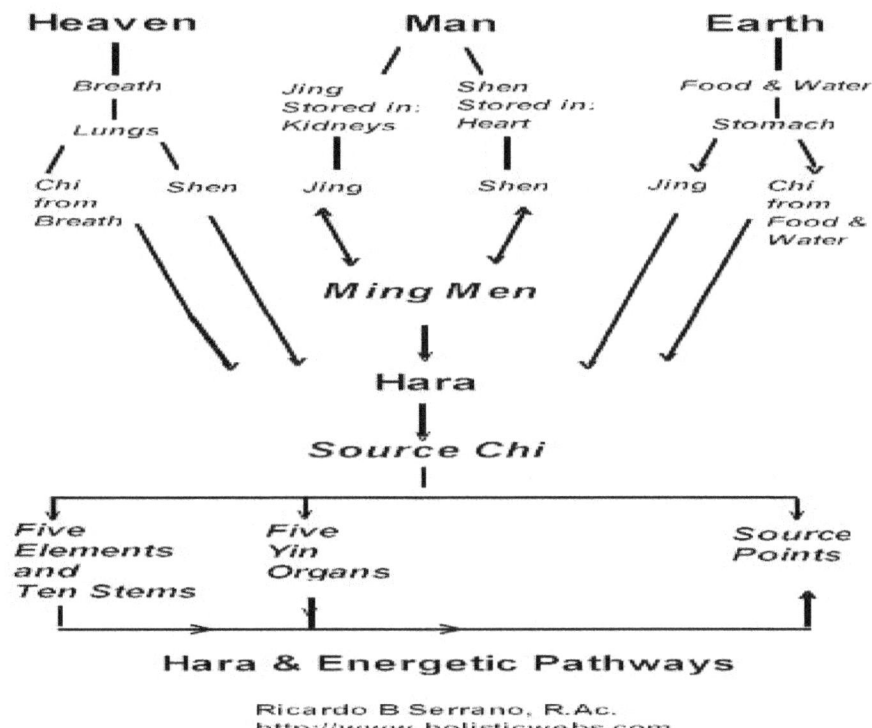

Hara & Energetic Pathways

The Nan Ching theory of energetic anatomy is centered in the Hara. The energetic nourishment of Jing and Shen, the passage of Chi and maintenance of the pulse are not the only functions rooted in the Hara. The Gathering of Eminent Acupuncturists and the Compendium of Acupuncture and Moxibustion discuss how the Ten Stems relate to the Source points. At the same time they present another viewpoint on the relationship of Triple Warmer and Heart Main-Pericardium to the Ten Stems.

Recognition of the Hara as the "Root," the center, pervades the practice of acupuncture and all other ideas based on the classical concepts of health. As the center of the energetic system and the starting point from which many techniques of diagnosis and treatment are developed it completes or supplements the Five Elements system. The Hara itself is seen as an area that encompasses the whole abdomen. It is focused around the area called Chi Hai or Chi Hai Tanden which overlaps the Spleen and Kidney reflex areas centering around CV-5 and CV-6, the Ma Point of the Triple Warmer and the "Sea of Chi. Reference: Five Elements and Ten Stems by Kiiko Matsumoto and Stephen Birch, 19

Wing Chun and Qigong by Ricardo B Serrano

Wing Chun forms cultivate and develop Qi energy and power. – Sifu Samuel Kwok

Since I was a kid, I was attracted to the martial arts watching my favorite Jeet Kune Do master Bruce Lee. His style and action movies piqued my interest to study all styles of martial arts from *karate*, *aikido* and *wing chun*. The other important reason for my martial arts studies is to defend myself from so many bullies in the Philippines where I grew up and in Canada where I worked and retired.

Create a bridge if the opponent's bridge is not present. – Wing Chun Maxim, see page 81

I studied with Lama Tantrapa's *Qi Dao* that included martial arts Qigong together with other styles of Qigong. I also studied with *Sheng Zhen* Qigong Master Li Jun Feng and *Wuji Qigong* Master Michael Winn. *Kundalini awakening* taught by Sri Vidya teacher Raja Choudhury is a good adjunct to Qigong. I'm now practicing Wing Chun with my wooden dummy because I find that with *Chi Sao*, *Siu Lim Tao* form and other forms altogether cultivate and develop Qi energy in the *lower dantian* to deliver *Fa Jing* (one inch) fist strike power as taught by *Sifu Samuel Kwok*. Its economy of motion, center line principle, defensive arm movements with strikes and kicks are ideal for close body self-defense that work.

The *Ip Man Wing Chun system* has today become one of the most popular martial art systems in the world. Bruce Lee was initially responsible for bringing Wing Chun to the attention of the world, but it has been through the teaching of today's masters, and most notably Ip Man's sons *Ip Chun* and *Ip Ching* that we have full knowledge of the heritage of this great Kung Fu system.

Sifu Samuel Kwok said, "*when you enter a life-death fight, you will not have your family or certificate that will set you up (in the case of your war art education). So stop talking and work hard.*"

It is good to understand this approach, especially in this community where many people eat each other about the genocide and various communities. When the work is over, it will not matter what our documents are, but who we are. They say a good student is hard to find, but a good master is much harder to find. I think I can't get a chance to be with many beautiful masters such as my precious Sifu. Have confidence of your Martial Arts/ Kung fu if you do it correctly. Doesn't matter how big and strong your opponents are. Train hard and keep an open mind. *Grandmaster Ip Man* was only 5'3".

The *wooden dummy* helps Wing Chun practitioners avoid using force against force and for learning the 116 movements. It's also a powerful training device to help develop stamina, balance, accuracy, timing, mobility and positioning. *Chi Sao* is not a drill but is considered as light sparring to learn how to gauge sensitivity as well as applying techniques and theories learned in the hand forms to fight better. The practice of Wing Chun and Qigong forms both have health and life-saving self-defense benefits.

Dantien Sitting Qigong
Enlightenment Qigong Mastery Center
http://www.enlightenmentqigong.com

Cultivating Qi in the Hara and Its Energetic Pathways (2)

"When you have a disease, do not try to cure it. Find your center and you will be healed.

There are some things that can be sensed but not explained in words."

-- Taoist proverbs

"You connect with the power of now and end suffering when you are centered in your Hara -- the center of Self or True Essence of Being." -- Ricardo B Serrano

Qigong healers and meditation masters use this Hara (Dantien) Sitting Qigong technique -- a Taoist form of lower dantien breathing combined with postures -- for self-healing (insomnia, low energy, digestive problems, etc) improving organ functions, quieting the mind, inner peace, internal martial arts application, centered and present in the power of now, expanded awareness, joy, and cultivating Qi energy for blissful enlightenment.

Why does the Hara (Dantian) sitting Qigong work? From a Taoist qigong point of view, it works because the Three Treasures Jing, Qi and Shen are cultivated. The Jing (essence) and Yuan Qi (vitality) stored in dantian and lower energy centers and gathered through the practice of Hara (Dantian) sitting Qigong and various Enlightenment Qigong forms with Chinese tonic herbs supplementation are utilized by the higher energy centers to develop the Shen (Spirit) energy.

"By leaving behind the chest-out-belly in posture and attitude of the West and adopting the belly-centered posture and attitude of Hara, individuals can live a calm, grounded, and more balanced life." -- Karlfried Graf Durckheim, Hara: The Vital Center of Man

According to Karlfried Durckheim's Hara: The Vital Center of Man, "Hara implies for the Japanese all that he considers essential to man's character and destiny. Hara is the center of the human body. It is at the same time the center in a spiritual sense or, to be more accurate, a nature given spiritual sense."

The man with belly is centered, tranquil, balanced. He is "large minded, one who is magnanimous and warm hearted."

Conversely, the man without a belly lacks calm judgement. He reacts haphazardly and capriciously.

He is easily startled and nervous... he lacks that inner axis which would prevent his being thrown off center. "The man with no belly is in every respect a picture of immaturity."

Traditionally then for the Japanese, hara, the belly, meant strength, maturity and a tranquil mind.

Al Huang in his book Embrace Tiger, Return to Mountain describes the difference between the Oriental and the Western man:

"The Oriental man is very empty and light up here in the head and very heavy down here in the belly and he feels very secure. The Western man is light in the belly and very heavy up here in the head, so he topples over."

In Tai Chi Chuan, Qigong and other eastern martial arts the center of gravity (Aikido with Ki) is located in the lower belly, and the reservoir of Life Energy or Breath Energy is also in the lower belly. From this "single spot in the lower abdomen" movement begins and energy is made. This spot is revered as the source of life in man. In Taoist yoga it is pictured as a burning cauldron producing the energy needed to open up and liberate the rest of the body.

NOTE: To have and maintain a powerful rooting and grounding like a tree, the middle (heart center) and upper dantians (ni-wuan) are aligned with the Hara (lower dantian). The three dantians are all important because without alignment and activation of the three dantians, the power and stability of the TaiJi pole in the center of the body cannot be manifested and maintained.

To energetically align yourself with the universal Qi or become one with universal Qi of heaven and earth -- experience Qigong state, lower dantien breathing with awareness of the three dantians aligned must be integrated with the postures or movements of Tai Chi, Qigong or eastern martial arts because when our practice harmonizes breath, postures or movements and hara (lower dantian) meditation we become Self-realized beings at one with the Dao.

"Our mind is always thinking of something, but with meditation, through relaxing the mental aspect we can harmonize ourselves with our true nature, the microcosm, and experience the universe, the macrocosm. This is what we call the Tao." -- Sun Do Master Hyunmoon Kim

It would be difficult to overstate the importance of the Dantian. Any question of its centrality to life and health is obviated by Chi Po's answer to the Yellow Emperor in the Nan Jing:

"The Yellow Emperor asked: 'The pulse is normal, and yet sometimes people die, why is this?'

Chi Po answered, 'Each of the twelve meridians has a relationship to the vital energies, the living Qi. The source of the vital energies is the root-origin of the twelve meridians and the Moving Qi between the kidneys, the Dantian. This means that the source of the vital energies is fundamental to the five Yin and six Yang organs, the root of the twelve meridians, the gate of breathing. It is the source of or origin of the Triple Warmer. Another name for it is the Protecting Shen Against Evil; and therefore Qi is the root of the person. This is why if the root is dying, the Stems and Branches (meridians and organs) will be dying, yet appear normal. The vital Qi is dying inside, but it is still there on the outside (the pulse is normal).'"

Tancheon or Lower Dantian Breathing

Psychological stability and healing is difficult and requires practicing correct breathing. Earth energy and heaven energy meet in the lower dantian. The lower dantian generates energy and is similar to an electric generator. Energy is generated by the lower dantian and becomes the source of thinking, talking, and acting.

Distracted thinking and worrying are dissipated when you focus your mind on the lower dantian. Correct lower dantian breathing provides a person with energy. When the energy is full then the head becomes clear and the heart gets brighter.

When the body is charged with vitality the mind gets clear and the heart becomes brighter.

When the mind is clear the body becomes lively and vitality is abundant. Tancheon or Lower Dantian Breathing is a method that produces mental and physical health by working with the body, mind, and heart.

The body's vitality is called jing centered in the lower dantian. The power that makes mental activity possible is called Qi. The energy of the heart is called shen. All three spread throughout the whole body.

The relationship between them can be compared to a candle. Jing is the candlestick, Qi is the flame, and Shen is the light that emanates from the flame. The flame becomes greater when the candlestick is bigger. The light is brighter when the flame is greater.

Thus, when Jing is abundant Qi becomes greater and when Qi is great Shen becomes brighter. The basic principle of Sun Do Tancheon or Lower Dantian breathing practice is to make Jing abundant, Qi greater, and Shen brighter.

According to Kiiko Matsumoto's Hara Diagnosis: Reflections on the Sea, "We can see here an immediate and simple diagnosis, the examination of the breathing ability. If the breathing is shallow and does not reach into the abdomen, the nourishment that the moving Qi needs is not adequate. Practice of deep breathing is therapeutically useful, providing immediate relief and a source of energy for the moving Qi. The "gate of breathing" is an important Daoist concept.

We can understand ming men as a concept intimately involved with the Nan Jing idea of a gate of breathing. This also parallels the idea of the hun from heaven and po from earth entering at birth and returning to heaven and earth at death. Similarly, the source, the root of the twelve meridians, is the place where earth's energy reacts with heaven's energy. This may be why the meridians were named the twelve branches in relation to the cosmological concept of terrestrial branches. In effect, the source is the point of interaction for the cosmological energies that comprise men.

The moving Qi between the kidneys is the "shen that protects against evil." This establishes for us the relationship between the moving Qi and the shen that the classical texts tell us is stored in the heart. However, this idea is more intricate. In his commentary on this idea, Sosen Hirooka says:

The moving Qi is called the shen of protecting evil. This means heaven's Qi is in the person.

Inside the Qi, shen is created. This shen protects. It means that all kinds of evil cannot invade the person's body.

This attraction of "heaven Qi" into the person and the resultant creation of shen which protects the body is part of breathing. When breathing is correct, this process functions well. Like most concepts that relate to the source, this idea has multiple applications. Correct breathing may be utilized for good health and is the root of Daoist contemplative practices.

The moving Qi is also the origin of the triple warmer. According to the Nan Jing, this relationship is quite complex. The triple warmer transports source Qi from its origin to the source points of each of the twelve meridians. Chapter 66 of the Nan Jing states:

> The triple warmer is the alternative messenger of the source Qi.

Thus, it maintains the basic energetic connection of the twelve meridians to the source."

NOTE: Ricardo B Serrano, R.Ac. as a Qigong healer, tonifies his patients' hara (lower dantian) with his Qi-healing for a faster recovery of their chronic health problems.

For preventive health maintenance, stress management and spiritual awakening, breathing with postures, meditation and Qigong are taught to clients together with Qi- healing, acupuncture, acupressure and herbs mainly to cultivate the Three Treasures Jing, Qi and Shen.

Traditional Wing Chun Rules of Conduct
Remain disciplined – Conduct yourself ethically as a martial artist.
Practice courtesy and righteousness – Serve the society and respect your elders.
Love your fellow students – Be united and avoid conflicts.
Limit your desires and pursuit of bodily pleasures – Preserve the proper spirit.
Train diligently – Maintain your skills.
Learn to develop spiritual tranquility – Abstain from arguments and fights.
Participate in society – Be moderate and gentle in your manners.
Help the weak and the very young – Use martial skills for the good of humanity.
Pass on the tradition – Preserve this Chinese art and rules of conduct. See pages 72, 81 and 83

The Three Dantians

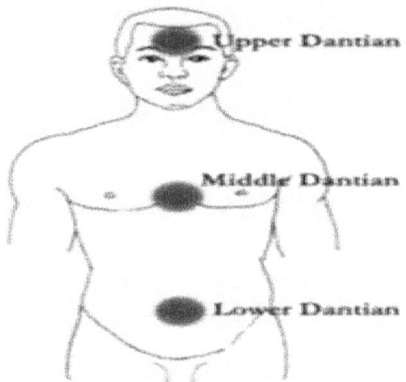

Sources:
Johnson, Jerry Alan. Chinese Medical Qigong Therapy. vol 1. Pacific Grove: The International Institute of Medical Qigong, 2005. 211-33. Print.

There are three major energy centers in the human body along the Taiji Pole (center channel) that store and emit energy. These Three energy centers in Ancient Daoist Energetic Anatomy and Physiology are called the three dantians. Located in the lower abdomen, chest, and head, each dantian has its own function and properties.

The Lower Dantian

The Lower Dantian is the center of physical strength and stamina and is located in the center of a triangle formed in your pelvic bowel by drawing a line from your perineum, navel, and mingmen (lower back). The lower dantian is also responsible for kinesthetic feeling, awareness, and communication. Expert martial artists learn to become familiar with this important energy center to feel and anticipate an opponent's attack. This energy center houses the mind that gets subconscious
feelings or "gut feelings" that the logical mind cannot process.

All Qigong training begins with focusing on the Lower Dantian in order to develop familiarity with remaining rooted by gathering the body's Qi and strengthening the foundation of the body's energy.

The Lower Dantian is considered the most yin energy center of the three dantians. This Dantian is closest to the Earth (yin) and is associated with the Jing (essence) and the physical energy of the body. Because the lower dantian is closest to the Earth it naturally gathers and stores the Earth's yin energy which counter balances the great yang energy cultivated during Qigong practice.

The first Wei Qi field (energy field) is associated with the lower dantian and is the closest to the physical tissue. Because the Lower Dantian represents Jing (essence) and matter, it is only natural that the first Wei Qi field only extends a few inches past the physical tissue.

The Middle Dantian

The Middle Dantian is the center of emotional energies in the human body and is located in the chest area. This Dantian is capable of emotional communication through the empathy of the heart, which means that one can read the emotions of another.

Often times Qigong practitioners will focus on training the Middle Dantian to release psycho-emotional patterns. If enough emotions are brought to surface suppressed memories of traumas, which created certain daily behavior and emotional patterns, will manifest. In doing this a Qigong Practitioner will choose to address these issues by intercepting karma, taking responsibility, and projecting no blame. Then the healing occurs in the main organ related to the Middle Dantian, the heart. The heart is responsible for forgiveness and is the final stage of healing after addressing all emotions and boundaries created by traumas. This type of practice will often times bring about ego or spiritual deaths where a practitioner will completely change their life, change their energetic resonance and change friends, and increase energetic potential for it takes energy to suppress emotions.

The Second Wei Qi field is associated with the Middle Dantian and manifests roughly two to three feet distance from the physical tissue. For people who see Auras, this is the Wei Qi field in which the colors of emotions are seen within.

The Upper Dantian

The Upper Dantian is the center for intuitive awareness, psychic abilities, and spiritual Communications. Daoist Mystics and Alchemists have interest in the Upper Dantian for the Crystal Chamber in which is where psychic perceptions take place. Even though psychic abilities take place here, it is necessary to have all Three Dantians balanced for a more proper and effective perceptions

When peaceful, tranquil, and not disrupted by emotional troubles of the subconscious mind, a Qigong student can intuitively process information taken in by the universe.
This ability is to "know without knowing" and is useful for observing the subconscious patterns of the practitioner and others.

Because the Upper Dantian is related to the Shen (spirit) as well as the 6th, 7th, and 8th chakras, it is used to spirit travel.

The Third Wei qi Field is associated with the Upper Dantian and manifests from six feet to infinite space. The Upper Dantian is related to Shen (spirit) and thought.

Caution: Do not practice Shen Gong exercises to open psychic abilities and intuitive awareness without first training the Lower Dantian to root to avoid self induced energetic psychosis.

Keys of Wing Chun Kuen (see Wing Chun and Qigong, page 72)
    Be ferocious when clashing.
    Be fast with your fist.
    Be forceful when applying power.
    Be accurate with timing.
    Be continuous when applying Fan Sau (the continued controlling & attacking an opponent)
    Do not use all your strength.
    Protect your own posture.
    Be alert with your eyes.
    Unite your waist and stance.
    Coordinate your hands and feet.
    Movements must be agile.
    Comprehend the principles of Yin and Yang.
    Remain calm.
    Be steady with your breathing and strength.
    Sink your inner chi.
    Be commanding with your fighting demeanor.
    Be quick to end the fight.

Maxims of Wing Chun Kuen (see Wing Chun Training Proverbs, page 83)
Retain what comes in, send off what retreats. Rush in on loss of hand contact.
Do not be lax when your opponent is not advancing.
Once your opponent moves, his center of gravity changes.
Make the first move to have control. Attack according to timing.
Timing is achieved through practice.
A strong attitude and posture give an advantage over your opponent.
Being alert and adapting to the situation allows maximum results for minimum effort.
The body follows the movement of the hands. The waist and the stance move together.
Complement the hands with posture to make good use of the centerline.
The eyes and the mind travel together, paying attention to leading edge of attack.
Charge into the opponent. Execute three moves together.
Strike any presented posture if it is there. Otherwise strike where you see motion. Beware of sneak attacks, leakage attacks and invisible centerline attacks.
Soft and relaxed strength will put your opponent in jeopardy.
Coordinate the hands and feet. Movement is together.
Do not take risks and you will always connect to the target.
Have confidence and your calmness will dominate the situation.
Occupy the inner gate to strike deep into the defense.
To win in an instant is a superior achievement.
The Yin Yang principle should be thoroughly understood.
Be humble to request your teacher for guidance. Understand the principles for your training.
The three terrors of Wing Chun are Tan Sau, Bong Sau, and Fok Sau; with Huen Sau, Gaun Sau.

Chinese Medical Qigong Therapy

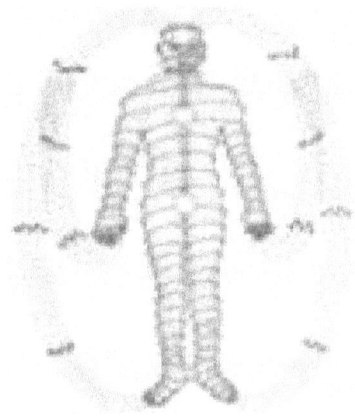

"The body is enveloped by Qi, or electromagnetic currents, affecting both internal and external organ functions."
– International Institute of Medical Qigong

According to Chinese Medical Qigong Therapy, "Qigong is a powerful system of healing and energy medicine from China. Qi means "Life-force energy" and gong means "skill," so Qigong (pronounced Chigong) is the skillful practice of gathering, circulating, and applying life-force energy. It uses breathing techniques, gentle movement, and meditation to cleanse, strengthen, and circulate the life energy or Qi and leads to better health and vitality and a tranquil state of mind. The primary goal is to purge toxic emotions from within the body's tissues, eliminate energetic stagnations, as well as strengthen and balance the internal organs and energetic fields.

All living bodies generate an external field of energy called Wei Qi (pronounced "whey chee"), which translates as "protective energy." The definition of Wei Qi in Medical Qigong is slightly different than that of Traditional Chinese Medicine (TCM). In classical TCM texts, the Wei Qi field is seen to be limited to the surface of the body, circulating within the tendon and muscle tissues. In Medical Qigong, however, the Wei Qi field also includes the three external layers of the body's auric and subtle energy fields. This energy originates from each of the internal organs and radiates through the external tissues. There the Wei Qi forms an energy field that radiates from the entire physical body. This field of Qi protects the body from the invasion of external pathogens and communicates with, as well as interacts with, the surrounding universal and environmental energy fields.

Both internal and external pathogenic factors affect the structural formation of the Wei Qi. The internal factors include suppressed emotional influences (such as anger and grief from emotional traumas). The external factors include environmental influences when they are too severe or chronic, such as Cold, Damp, Heat or Wind, etc. Physical traumas also affect the Wei Qi field.

Any negative interchange affects the Wei Qi by literally creating holes within the matrix of the individual's external energetic fields. When left unattended, these holes leave the body vulnerable to penetration, and disease begins to take root in the body. Strong emotions, in the form of toxic energy, become trapped within the body's tissues when we hold back or do not integrate our feelings. These unprocessed emotions block the natural flow of Qi, thus creating stagnant pools of toxic energy within the body.

Medical Qigong consists of specific techniques that uses the knowledge of the body's internal and external energy fields to purge, tonify, and balance these energies. Medical Qigong therapy offers patients a safe and effective way to rid themselves of toxic pathogens and years of painful emotions that otherwise, can cause mental and physical illness. This therapy combines breathing techniques with movement, creative visualization, and spiritual intent to improve health, personal power, and control over one's own life."

Wing Chun Training Proverbs

There are two main points in Chum Kiu: to avoid [attacks] by turning, and to be stable. - Ip Chun
There are not many sets of training exercises in Wing Chun. They are easy to learn but to master them requires determination. Learning the usual ways will allow later variations. Short arm bridges and fast steps require practicing the stance first. *Siu Lim Tao* mainly trains internal power. Lan Sao in *Chum Kiu* (seeking the bridge) is a forceful technique with movement and turning, footwork, hand blocks and kicks, and builds on Siu Lim Tao. *Biu Jee (darting fingers)* form contains life saving emergency techniques: inch jing energy, footwork, Kop Jarn or downward elbow, and Biu Gee/Tse. The Wooden Man develops use of power. Fancy techniques should not be used in sticky hand practice. Sticky leg practice is inseparable from the single leg stance. The steps follow turning of the body like a cat. The posture complements the hands to eject the opponent. The Six and a Half Point Staff does not make more than one sound. The Eight Cut Sword techniques have no match. The thrusting and fast attacks are well suited for closing in. Eyes beaming with courage can neutralize the situation. Those who completely master the system are among the very few. See *Wing Chun & Qigong*, p. 72; *Maxims*, p. 81

Chinese Tonic Herbs to Cultivate Jing, Qi and Shen

"There is nothing which heaven does not cover, yet nothing that earth does not sustain." -- Chuang Tzu

There needs to be a balance and integration between the heavenly yang therapies such as Qi-healing, Qigong and acupuncture with the earthly yin aspect such as diet and tonic superior herbs which together create harmony, healing wholeness of yin and yang and spiritual oneness with the universe to truly envision what Taoist master Chuang Tzu said, "There is nothing which heaven does not cover, yet nothing that earth does not sustain."

Tonic herbs are herbs which promote a long, healthy, vibrant, happy life without any unwanted side effects even when taken over a long period of time. The tonic or Superior Herbs, essentially, are empowering and healthful "super-foods" which benefit our well being in ways that more common foods cannot. And they have a protective, balancing, vitalizing quality beyond that of any other herbs. They are generally consumed as a herbal supplement to a well balanced healthy diet for the purpose of optimizing our nutritional needs.

Applying the principle of the Three Treasures is the highest form of great herbalism. In the Orient it is called "the Superior Herbalism." Six tonic or superior herbs revered by the great sages as the quintessential substances to cultivate the Three Treasures (Qi, Shen, and Jing) are Reishi mushrooms, Ginseng, Schizandra fruit (Wu Wei Zi), Asparagus Root (Tian Men Dong), Gynostemma Pentaphyllum (Jiao Gu Lan), and Rhodiola (Hong Jing Tian). Before we describe their herbal properties, Shen Nong Ben Cao (Divine Farmer's Materia Medica) and Huang Di Neijing (Yellow Emperor's Classic of Medicine) described them as superior or immortal foods as opposed to the medicinal and radical herbs:

Huang Di asked, "Can you tell me about the three grades of herbs that were recorded in the Shen Nong Ben Cao (Shen Nong's Materia Medica)?"

Qi Bo replied, "In ancient times the art of herbology was practiced by categorizing all herbs into three classifications. The first category of herbs was called superior, or immortal foods because of their lack of side effects and strengthening qualities. These were often incorporated into one's diet and were used as preventive measures. The second category of herbs was called medium or medicinal and were used to rectifying imbalances in the human body. These were used until the patient recovered from their illness and then withdrawn. The third category of herbs was called inferior or radical herbs, so named because they are strong in action and not without side effects; sometimes they are toxic. Therefore these were used often in small amounts and once the desired action took place they were discontinued immediately.

"The paramount mission in healing is to dispel the pathogen and strengthen the patient."

The first superior class section of 6 herbs listed in the Shen Nong Ben Cao Jing which have been left out of the mainstream of TCM training and practice are none other than six different colors of Ling Zhi (Ganoderma), commonly known as Reishi Mushroom. These six varieties of Reishi are related to the 5 elements. Green, Red, Yellow, White, Black, and are related to Wood, Fire, Earth, Metal, and Water, while the 6th Reishi, Purple, zi zhi, is not explained clearly. Since Purple Rieshi is rather difficult to find, this is a truly sublime substance which was used in Taoist practices to open the heart, and could be categorized under the fire element.

In its description of almost all the superior quintessential substances to cultivate shen, qi and jing, especially Reishi, the Ben Cao describes the substances in this way:

"Protracted taking may make the body light, prevent senility, and prolong life so as to make one an immortal."

The Reishi mushroom, also known by its formal name of Ganoderma and its Chinese name Ling Zhi, has attained an unparalleled reputation in the Orient as the ultimate herbal substance. For over three thousand years it has been the most sought-after product of nature by mountain sages and by the emperors and empresses of all Eastern nations. In the first Chinese herbal text (Shen Nong's Pharmacopeia) written about 2400 years ago, Reishi was classified as a "superior herb" which is defined as one that "serves to maintain life, promote radiant health and long life because of its normalizing action, and to cause no side effects, even when used continuously." That ancient book said that "continuous consumption of Reishi makes your body light and young, lengthens your life and turns you into one like the immortal who never dies." Thus Reishi was traditionally called "the mushroom of immortality."

The Reishi Mushroom grows wild only upon old trees and roots of certain types of trees in remote mountain forests of China, Japan and Korea. Only in the fifteen years have we seen the cultivation of Reishi, and thus the commercial availability of this amazing health product. Reishi has been the object of intensive scientific studies to discern its many health functions from a modern perspective. Traditionally, Reishi is believed to be a tonic to all of the body's energies. It was revered as a major tonic to each of the three Treasures, Jing, Qi and Shen.

As a Jing (Essence) tonic, Reishi is believed to have major life lengthening effects when consumed over a long period of time. It is believed to build primal power and to replenish energy spent handling stressful situations.

As a Qi (Vitality) tonic, Reishi is used to build energy, although it is slightly sedative in the short run. It is most famous as an herb used to build the immune system. Many studies done in Japan have shown Reishi to have a powerful effect on the body's overall resistance to disease. Reishi is believed by Japanese and Chinese researchers to have a regulatory effect on the immune system, bringing up immune functions in cases of immunodeficiency and reducing the excesses associated with auto-immune conditions. Reishi is a superb tonic for people who suffer from chronic allergies. Reishi is also believed to have major benefits on the lungs and liver. Studies done in Japan have shown that Reishi protects the liver from damage due to toxic chemicals, including pharmaceutical metabolites. Furthermore, studies done in Japan and elsewhere have also demonstrated that Reishi is beneficial to the cardiovascular system, since it appears to help regulate coronary and cerebral blood flow and also seems to help reduce levels of blood lipids and in lowering elevated cholesterol.

As a Shen (Spirit) tonic, nothing compares to Reishi. It is simply the greatest Shen tonic of them all. It is believed by the Chinese to protect the Spirit and to nurture the growth of intelligence, wisdom and spiritual insight. Reishi is a superb anti-stress herb. Everyone who takes Reishi notices the peacefulness that seems to accompany its use. Many people are able to stop using chemical drugs. And Reishi seems to be cumulative, gradually strengthening the nerves and actually changing how we perceive life. It has routinely been used by mountain hermits, monks, Daoist adepts and spiritual seekers throughout Asia because it was believed to help calm the mind, ease tension, strengthen the nerves, improve memory, sharpen concentration and focus, build will power and, as a result, help build wisdom. That is why it was called the "Mushroom of Spiritual Potency" by these seekers. The people of Asia believe more than ever in Reishi's power to improve the quality of life by improving the inner life of a human being. All the scientific validation only explains the physical nature of Reishi, but it is the profound ability of Reishi to improve one's life on every plane that makes it so incredible.

Studies done in Asia indicate that Reishi is a supreme health food supplement that has virtually no toxicity or side effects.

There are many Reishi products coming to the market at this time, but very few are truly excellent. Reishi must be extracted to be digestible and assimilable. Unfortunately, most Reishi products are not extracted and most are made from inferior quality hot house mushrooms or use inferior cultivated Ganoderma mycelium.

Other Common Names
Reishi mushroom, Ling Zhi, Ganoderma
Pharmaceutical Latin: Ganoderma Pinyin:
Ling Zhi

Treasures: Jing, Qi and Shen
Atmospheric Energy: Neutral or slightly warm
Organ Meridian Systems: Heart, Liver, Lungs, Kidney
Part Used and Form: Fruiting body, spores, mycelium

Primary Functions
Nourishing tonic, tonic to the three treasures (Jing, Qi and Shen), builds body resistance, detoxifying, aphrodisiac, sedative, prolongs life and enhances intelligence and wisdom

Qualities
Ganoderma is arguably the most revered herbal substance in Asia, certainly ranking with ginseng as the elite substance for the attainment of radiant health, longevity and spiritual attainment. It has maintained that position for at least 2000 years, and its reputation and value are only increasing. Numerous legends provide a rich and extensive record of Ganoderma in Asian society.

Reishi has traditionally been used as an anti-aging herb and has been used for many diseases and disorders as well. It has long been a favorite tonic food supplement by the Chinese Royal family and virtually any one who could obtain it. Ganoderma was particularly revered by the followers of the Taoist tradition as the "Elixir of Immortality." Taoists have continuously claimed that Reishi promotes calmness, centeredness, balance, inner awareness and inner strength. They have used it to improve meditative practices and to protect the body, mind and spirit so that the adept could attain both a long and healthy life and spiritual immortality. Due to its rarity, the common people could rarely obtain a Reishi mushroom, but it was popularly revered as a greater treasure than any jewel.

Since Reishi has been known to have many functions, it has been the subject of a great deal of research in recent years. It is absolutely safe, being non-toxic. It ranks in Asia with Ginseng, Deer Antler, Astragalus and Cordyceps as a pre-eminent tool in the attainment of radiant health.

Its health benefits of Reishi are extremely broad and it is virtually non-toxic. Though it is now used much like ginseng, Eleutherococcus and Astragalus as a general tonic to help develop energy, to improve digestion and to improve sleep, scientists are exploring its potential in their terms

Ganoderma is a profound immune potentiator. It has been found to significantly improve the functioning of the immune system whether the immune system is deficient or excessive. In this sense, it is an immune "modulator" --- that is, it helps to modulate, or regulate, and fine tune the immune system. Our immune system is a virtually miraculous network of activities designed over millions of years to protect us from viruses, bacteria, parasites, molds, dust, pollen and malignant cells. It is the responsibility of the immune system to detect the intrusion, or invasion, of these entities and to mount a defense in order to eliminate them. A healthy immune system is capable of resisting most such intruders and a very hardy system may be able to resist invasions that many other people's systems cannot. If the immune system is weakened or malfunctioning, the invading microbes can easily establish a foothold in our body and disease sets in. Antibiotics can often be used to stop the invasion at this time, but chronic use of antibiotics further weakens the immune response. Furthermore, antibiotics are useless against viruses, pollens and most parasites. They are certainly useless against malignant (cancerous) cells generated in our own bodies. It is much better to resist the invasion from within with a fully fortified immune system and not become ill in the first place. This is where herbs like Reishi our now attracting the attention of scientists and consumers alike.

Many chemical constituents play a role in GL's immune modulating capacity. The polysaccharide components in particular seems to play an important role in attacking cancerous cells, but not healthy ones, while simultaneously strengthening the body's overall immune functions. The polysaccharides appear to help the body attack microbial invaders such as viruses, bacteria and yeast.

But Reishi does not just "stimulate" the immune system. It regulates it. And that is what makes Reishi so precious. If the immune system is excessive, as is the case with auto-immune diseases and allergies, Reishi can have significant positive influence. A group of chemicals known as the ganoderic acids help fight auto-immune diseases such as allergies. Ganoderic acids inhibit histamine release, improve oxygen utilization and improve liver functions. Ganoderic acids are also potent antioxidant free-radical scavengers.

Still another component, Beta-1, 3-glucan, helps regulate and stabilize blood sugar levels. Not only that, but these same components have been shown to have powerful anti-tumor properties.

Reishi is widely used in Asia to improve the cardiovascular system. It helps lower HDL (the "bad" cholesterol) and reduce excess fatty acids. It has been found to prevent and treat hardening of the arteries, angina and shortness of breath associated with coronary heart disease.

In 1977 it was discovered in Japan that Reishi had potent anti-cancer activity. It was first used to treat, and quite successfully, hairy-cell leukemia, which is caused by a retrovirus closely related to HIV, the virus that causes AIDS. It has been an approved drug for cancer in Japan since that time and has been used safely and effectively, often in conjunction with other drugs or radiation. It has been demonstrated that Reishi can help reduce the side-effects of many kinds of chemotherapy and radiation treatment and simultaneously contribute to the rebuilding of the immune system---an essential part of the recovery from cancer. Ganoderma stimulates the production of interferon and interleukins I and II, all being potent natural anti-cancer substances produced in our own bodies. Reishi may well prove to be the greatest prevention against cancer because it helps us to protect ourselves by our own power. It has also been approved in Japan and China for the treatment of myasthenia gravis, a serious auto-immune disease. Besides that, it is commonly prescribed by MD.'s in Japan for chronic bronchitis, memory loss, insomnia, hyperlipidemia and a whole range of degenerative diseases of the elderly, including disorders associated with senility.

Reishi is a superb anti-stress herb. Throughout history it has been used to bring balance into the lives of people who needed help in this department, and that means most everyone. Deep in antiquity, it was routinely used by mountain hermits, monks, Taoist adepts and spiritual seekers throughout Asia because it was believed to help calm the mind, ease tension, strengthen the nerves, strengthen memory, sharpen concentration, improve focus, build will power and, as a result, help build wisdom. That is why it was called the "Mushroom of Spiritual Potency" by these seekers. The people of Asia have never lost their faith in Reishi. They believe more than ever in Reishi's power to improve the quality of life by improving the inner life of a human being. All the scientific validation only explains the physical nature of Reishi, but it is the profound ability of Reishi to improve one's life on every plane that makes it so miraculous. Reishi is indeed calming and centering. Everyone who takes Reishi notices the peacefulness that seems to accompany its use. Many people are able to stop using chemical drugs. And Reishi seems to be cumulative, gradually strengthening the nerves and actually changing how we perceive life.

Reishi is a substance that builds health on all levels. It is the rarest of jewels in Nature. Life itself is based on the ability to adapt to the stresses, the attacks, the challenges that come our way every day. Reishi seems to provide an incredible resource of the full range of energies we need to meet these challenges. Reishi is indeed "the great protector," protecting us on every level -- physically, immunologically, mentally, spiritually. It helps us adapt to the world and provides additional power for us to achieve a superior level of life. When we are so protected and so provided for, we can achieve things that otherwise would be impossible. That is why Reishi has been called the "herb of good fortune."

Panax Ginseng

One of the most famous and valued herbs used by mankind, Asian Ginseng is an energy tonic that regulates the human energy system. It has been shown to be stimulating and regulatory to both the central nervous system and to the endocrine system. It is the primary Qi tonic of Chinese tonic herbalism.

Ginseng helps a person to adapt to all kinds of stresses, and enhances endurance and resilience under stressful conditions. It has thus been termed an "adaptogenic" substance by scientific researchers. Ginseng is also used to tonify digestive and respiratory functions. In Chinese health practice, there is a theory of Li Qi, which literally means balance of energy. It is a term often used to describe the ability of Ginseng to balance the system at a fundamental level. In modern terms, this concept refers to the ability of Ginseng to help regulate body functions, or to strengthen the functions that regulate other body functions. On the basis of its pharmacological properties, Ginseng has been classified as and adaptogen.

Ginseng contains many active ingredients, but the most important are the saponins called ginsenosides. Ginsenosides specifically improve adaptability and are believed to help build muscle and endurance. Therefore Ginseng is very popular with athletes. Asian Ginseng generally has a "warm" energy.

Ginseng increases physical and mental efficiency, and has been shown to improve the accuracy of work by promoting concentration. Ginseng prevents overfatigue. High quality Ginseng is not a stimulant like amphetamines or caffeine, and it does not create nervousness or disturb sleep, yet it increases alertness.

Ginseng is used by Chinese traditional doctors as a tonic for general weakness, poor appetite, low sex drive, shortness of breath, cold limbs, spontaneous sweating and premature aging.

Ginseng is a superb herb for aged people. It has a mental stimulant effect in elderly persons and it improves memory and cognitive power, and can often reverse intellectual and mental deterioration. It quickens thinking and improves physical energy, often to a startling degree. Ginseng is very effective in hastening the recovery from illness and surgery.

There are in fact many varieties of Ginseng, all of which have distinct characteristics. Most high quality ginseng is good for men and women alike. Wild and semi-wild Ginseng is generally far superior to the cultivated, commercial varieties. The higher the quality, the more Shen (Spirit) a ginseng root is said to contain. There are also a number of superb sources of cultivated Ginseng, which have long traditions of excellence.

Generally, Ginseng is used with other herbs. However, Ginseng is often used by itself or with just one or two other herbs. Several varieties of Ginseng may be blended to create remarkable adaptogenic formulations.

Other Common Names: Ginseng Root

Pharmaceutical Latin: Panax Ginseng

Pinyin: Ren Shen

Treasures: Qi, Shen and Jing

Atmospheric Energy: Slightly Warm

Taste: Sweet, Slightly Bitter,

Organ Meridian Systems: Spleen and Lungs

Part Used and Form: Root (leaves are sometimes used as a tea)

Primary Functions: Tonify Qi, Adaptogenic, immune modulator, prolong life, overcome fatigue, increase blood volume, aid in recovery from illness or trauma, sharpen and calm the mind, stabilize the emotions, counteract stress and enhance wisdom

Qualities: On the basis of its pharmacological properties, Ginseng has been classified as and adaptogen. It is a powerful anti-stress agent. In Chinese health practice, there is a theory of Li Qi, which literally means balance of energy. It is a term often used to describe the ability of Ginseng to balance the system at a fundamental level. In modern terms, this concept refers to the ability of Ginseng to help regulate body functions, or to strengthen the functions that regulate other body functions.

Ginseng is used by Chinese traditional doctors as a tonic for general weakness, poor appetite, low sex drive, shortness of breath, cold limbs, spontaneous sweating and premature aging. Generally, Ginseng is used with other herbs. However, Ginseng is often used by itself or with just one or two other herbs.

Ginseng increases physical and mental efficiency, and has been shown to improve the accuracy of work by promoting concentration. Ginseng prevents overfatigue. Ginseng is not a stimulant like amphetamines or caffeine, yet it increases alertness. However, it does not provoke subjective excitation (nervousness) nor does it disturb sleep. It is, in fact, used in a great many sleep-aid formulations. In China, there is an almost universal practice by high school and college students to consume Ginseng during examination periods. The practice is generally to chew several pieces a day while preparing for examinations and to chew Ginseng constantly during the examination period. Students claim that it makes them more alert, helps them stay awake for days on end with little sleep and improves memory and reasoning ability.

This great herb has a mental stimulant effect in elderly persons. It improves memory and cognitive power and can often reverse intellectual and mental deterioration. It quickens thinking and improves physical energy, often to a startling degree. Ginseng is very effective in hastening the recovery from illness and surgery. Ginseng is a superb herb for aged people.

The tonic benefits of Ginseng are long lasting. When Ginseng is taken for an extended period of time, the physiological changes that take place as a result of the Ginseng last for a long period of time after the Ginseng is discontinued (if it is discontinued). Studies indicate, for example, that increased work efficiency is retained from one to two months after a one month course of Ginseng administration. People who take Ginseng to help regulate their blood sugar level will maintain normal blood sugar for several weeks after they discontinue Ginseng.

Many people claim that Ginseng has powerful aphrodisiac effects. The reputation as a sex tonic goes back to very ancient times. To this day, Ginseng maintains a reputation in this regard. I have known many men and women who have used Ginseng either for a short time or over long periods of time who claim that their sex lives improved noticeably after using Ginseng. Red Ginseng is most highly revered for its sex-stimulating qualities. Korean Ginseng in particular has a reputation for this. Ginseng certainly can help to improve sexual function by making both men and women stronger and more athletic. It improves endurance and muscular strength. By improving respiratory functions, sexual intercourse can be significantly lengthened. Sex is not merely a function of the gonads. The whole body must be healthy to enjoy sex to its fullest. However, Ginseng is believed to have gonadal effects as well. Men and women alike claim that Ginseng increases the urge for sex and intensifies sexual response.

Schizandra

The very name of Schizandra in Chinese tells us a great deal about the qualities of this herb. Wu Wei Zi means "Five Taste Fruit." Due to the fact that Schizandra possesses all five of the classical "tastes" (sour, bitter, sweet, spicy and salty) and thus possesses the essence of all five of the elemental energies (wood, fire, earth, metal and water), Schizandra is respected as a health-providing tonic in the same class with Ginseng and Ganoderma.

Schizandra has been used since the dawn of Chinese civilization as a tonic herb. From the beginning it has been revered, and remains one of the elite herbs of the Chinese system of herbalism. It was first written about in Shen Nong's Pharmacopoeia, where it was listed as a Superior herb. Ancient people considered Schizandra to be the quintessence of tonic herbs and the master of the five elements. Numerous stories and documents express that taking it often would help a person recover their youthful vigor and prolong their life. Schizandra was very popular with the emperors of China because it was believed that Schizandra added to sexual stamina, and since Chinese emperors always had many concubines, this was considered a primary asset. Chinese women historically held it in very high favor as well, especially the women of the imperial court, because of its beauty enhancing qualities. Taoists appreciated it because it was the quintessence of herbs helping to develop their spiritual power. Common people used it to promote vigor and alertness.

Asparagus Root
Wild Asparagus root is a marvelous Shen tonic and Yin tonic. It was credited by Chinese wise men as being able to open the heart, prolong life, and also to tonify the sexual functions of both men and women. It is traditionally used in Chinese herbalism as a major lung tonic. Prolonged consumption will make the skin soft, supple and smooth. In the art of radiant health, this kind of skin is a sure sign of attainment. Beautiful skin is the result of pure blood and healthy lungs. Asparagus root is useful for those who are experiencing dry skin due to a dry environment or due to internal dryness.

Thank You Note: The above information on the herbal properties of Reishi Mushroom, Panax Ginseng, Schizandra and Asparagus were taken from Ron Teeguarden's book Radiant Health, the Ancient Wisdom of the Chinese Tonic Herbs.

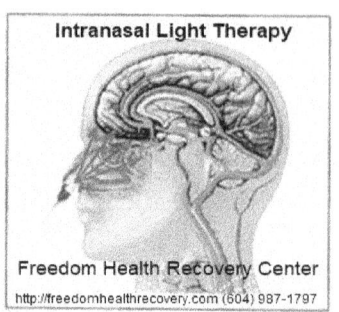

Intranasal Light Therapy involves the simple process of clipping a small red light diode to the nose to illuminate the nasal cavity. Researchers have found that this act initiates the process of healing a large number of health conditions such as high blood pressure, high cholesterol, diabetes and viral infection. How can such a simple device be so effective in healing so many diseases? In fact, the Intranasal Light Therapy device does only one thing, and it does it well. It stimulates the body to heal itself. The impact is systemic rather than directed at any particular condition. And in the process, many conditions are addressed.

Scientists who specialize in the stimulation characteristic of light (or "photobiomodulation") know that a certain wavelength of light can trigger the creation of singlet oxygen. At low dosage, these singlet oxygen particles settle into "Redox Signalling" molecules. These signalling molecules tell the body to line up its various elements to accomplish the following healing activities: activate the immune system, release antioxidants, increase blood flow, repair damaged DNA, and even encourage the death of damaged cells.

With Intranasal Light Therapy, this effect commences with the blood passing through the nasal region and then continues to spread throughout the body via the circulatory and lymphatic systems.

The reduction-oxidation ("redox") activities continuously take place inside the body, but when inflammation occurs due to an infection, or when cellular homeostasis (equilibrium of interdependent elements) is interrupted, the body's corrective system is called into action. The redox signalling (stimulated by light therapy as explained here) helps the body to more accurately direct this restorative action. The result is accelerated healing, or the body being put on alert.

There are no major side effects with this therapy. Nor does it require the introduction of a foreign substance into the body. The healing process is completely natural in harnessing the power of the body to repair itself. Intranasal Light Therapy is low-cost, effective and convenient, which makes it a healing breakthrough. It is a natural fit with the value system of naturopathic medicine. It does no harm, respects the natural power of the body to heal, addresses the causes of illness rather than the symptoms (at the molecular level), encourages self-responsibility for health, considers the fundamental health factors, and definitely promotes prevention of diseases. The above article was written by Dr. Lew Lim, ND, inventor of intranasal light therapy device. For more info on Intranasal Light Therapy, read *Why the health care system is broken*, page 138; *The Cure & Cause of Cancer*

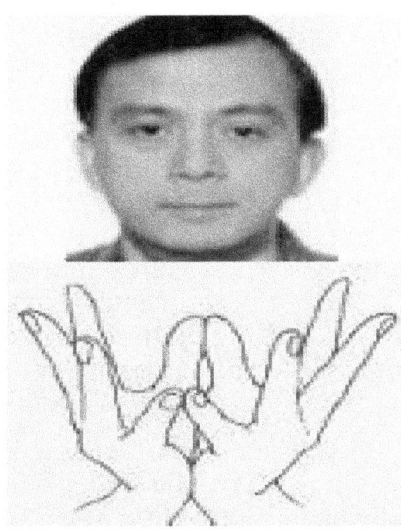

Ricardo B Serrano's Story

"True love is the recognition of the formless in the other -- which is the recognition of yourself in the other." – Eckhart Tolle

"Health and well-being can be achieved only by remaining centered in spirit, guarding against the squandering of energy, promoting the constant flow of qi and blood, maintaining harmonious balance of yin and yang, adapting to the changing seasonal and yearly macrocosmic influences, and nourishing one's self preventively. This is the way to a long and happy life." -- Huang Di Neijing

Working at the "Island Copper Mine" for 20 years followed by divorce and separation from my children took its toll on my health with symptoms of fatigue, high blood pressure, failing left eyesight with soreness, and depression.

I had acupuncture treatments, psychological counselling, pranic healing, diet and herbal medicine to resolve my persistent health problems during that time but nothing helped me to cure the symptoms permanently. So I reviewed my books Huang Di Neijing (Yellow Emperor's Classic of Medicine) and Shen Nong Ben Cao (Divine Farmer's Materia Medica) which mentioned Qigong and Chinese superior tonic herbs, the spiritual growth herbs. I also read Ron Teeguarden's book Radiant Health, the Ancient Wisdom of the Chinese Tonic Herbs which mentioned the saying in Chinese tonic herbalism that "it is all right to become fatigued, but never to become exhausted" and that "medicine and food are of the same origin" -- food is the best medicine and the best medicine is herbal and in particular the indispensable transformative tonic herbs which are the richest source of adaptogenic phytonutrients and immune-boosting antioxidants in the world. All these books mentioned about the necessity of cultivating the Three Treasures Shen (Spirit), Qi (vitality) and Jing (essence) in the body for holistic healing and returning to oneness by balancing the yin and yang, removing the pathogens and strengthening the body holistically through Qigong, acupuncture and Chinese superior tonic herbs as opposed to medicinal and inferior herbs.

Initially, nine years ago, I persistently learned and practiced Merkaba meditation from Master Alton Kamadon, Wuji Qigong from Taoist Master Michael Winn, Sheng Zhen Wuji Yuan Gong from Master Li Jun Feng, and finally became certified as a Pan Gu Mystical Qigong instructor from Master Ou Wen Wei. I have noticed that my symptoms of fatigue, depression and high blood pressure gradually went away for good but my failing left eye with soreness seemed to still bother me. I started using EFT therapy, Zhan Zhuang Qigong, Qi Dao, Shaktipat Meditation, and Guru Yoga with Master Choa Kok Sui's Super Brain Yoga which greatly relieved the eye pain.

Realizing that I have to balance my heavenly yang practices like Qigong with earthly yin Chinese tonic herbs, I started taking the three main Chinese tonic herbs Reishi Mushroom (Ling Zhi), Panax ginseng (Ren Shen) and Schizandra fruit (Wu Wei Zi) with other tonic herbs and Alkaline Water with Western herbs and intranasal light therapy which eventually took care of my left eye soreness and blurred vision. See Vagus Nerve Qi-healing, page 58

> When the shoe fits, the foot is forgotten.
> When the belt fits, the belly is forgotten.
> And when the Heart [shen] is right,
> "For" and "against" are forgotten.
> -- Chuang Tzu, Daoist sage

According to Ron Teeguarden's book Radiant Health, the Ancient Wisdom of the Chinese Tonic Herbs, "This passage expresses quite exquisitely an aspect of Chinese Taoist philosophy that is absolutely central to the attainment of health. Very simply, Chuang Tzu is saying that one cannot attain high spiritual levels until one has learned the art of balance. Those who seek true happiness must achieve balance in their lives. Imbalance is the source of stress that distracts shen's attention away from its higher path. But when there is balance and harmony in one's life, then the Heart, or shen has an opportunity to develop and attain a state of enlightened, all-embracing acceptance of things as they really are, transcending the notions of good and bad, right and wrong, for and against.

"The great Chinese tonic herbs are some of nature's sublime gifts. They can help the "shoe to fit," they can help the "belt to fit," and ultimately and most important, they can help the heart become "right," allowing us to rise above the illusionary world of duality and to know nature as it is, as a complete, unified, harmonious being, of which we a part.

"The tonic herbs can help restore that balance, harmony, and energy and are themselves the very essence of moderation. They can also help us sense our limits, to maintain our center, and to have the strength and wisdom to stop when we need to."

Nowadays, as a 69 year middle age natural healing exponent, I remain physically active regularly climbing 15 floors, swimming over ten laps in the pool, and walking uphill everyday to keep and maintain my health and stamina. Another unexpected benefit besides the improved vitality and immune system, and better adaptability to stressors that I have noticed with practicing Qigong, Dantien breathing with postures and meditation, and taking the Chinese tonic herbs which both cultivate my Three Treasures Shen, Qi and Jing) is the continuous experience of a sense of well-being, calmness, peace, overwhelming love, joy, and happiness which are all symptoms of oneness with the universe which I have longed for all these many years. Finally, I had come to a holistic understanding and validation of the Shiva Sutras of the Siddha Lineage of Kashmir Shaivism and of the Taoist concepts of Classical Chinese Medicine taught in the classical texts, Huang Di Neijing and Shen Nong Ben Cao, through my body-mind-spirit healing and spiritual experiences. Truth can only be known by experience, not by beliefs or thoughts.

"Health and well-being can be achieved only by remaining centered in spirit, guarding against the squandering of energy, promoting the constant flow of qi and blood, maintaining harmonious balance of yin and yang, adapting to the changing seasonal and yearly macrocosmic influences, and nourishing one's self preventively. This is the way to a long and happy life." -- Huang Di Neijing

Therefore, based from my personal natural holistic healing and life-saving experience and from my clients with stress -related disorders who benefited from the integrated modality of Qi-healing, Qigong, acupuncture, EFT and Chinese tonic herbs, I decided to initialize the Vancouver Qigong Mastery to share with the public and the fellow health practitioners in the palliative truncated Traditional Chinese Medicine and acupuncture profession its health-promoting longevity philosophy to heal stress-related disorders by returning to the 3,500-year-old ancient wisdom of classical Chinese art of radiant health by way of breathing with postures, meditation, Qigong, tonic herbalism, and acupuncture.

Thank you for reading this story of mine and my other Articles. May it's message benefit you in some way. May you have a long, happy and healthy life!

"The independent state of supreme consciousness is the reality of everything." - Shiva Sutra 1.1

This first sutra, caitanyamatma, states that individual being is one with universal being. The reality of this whole universe is God consciousness. It is filled with God consciousness.

In this sutra, the state of complete independence is indicated and accomplished through the use of the word caitanya... It is only this one aspect, svatantrya, that is revealed by the word caitanya. This indicates that the word caitanya means "the independent state of consciousness."

The independent state of consciousness is the self. It is the self of everything, because whatever exists in the world is the state of Lord Shiva. So Lord Shiva is found everywhere.

The joy of his samadhi is bliss for the whole universe. - Shiva Sutra 1.18

Whatever joy he feels while he is in samadhi is said to be the insertion of bliss for the whole universe. This yogi doesn't have to do anything. He only has to remain in samadhi and he will carry the whole universe into that supreme bliss.

According to Kashmir Shaivism teachings found in the Vijnana Bhairava, when a yogi resides with full awareness in the state of subjectivity, with the full joy of experiencing his own nature (camatkara), this is said to be the joy of his samadhi (mystical rapture).

There is another explanation of this sutra given by masters and that is, "Whenever this yogi, who is always residing in his own self (svatmarama), is introverted and established in his own self, then he naturally enjoys the bliss of samadhi. Anyone who sees this and thinks that this yogi is enjoying the bliss of samadhi will, at that very moment, also enter into samadhi. This is just like seeing a cobra not from distance, but face to face.

When you see a cobra and it bites you, you will be filled with the poison of that cobra. In the same way, when you observe a yogi who is established in the joy of samadhi and you understand that he is experiencing the joy of this samadhi, you will at once also relish the joy of samadhi. This reveals how this bliss is bestowed on the whole world.

-- Excerpted from Swami Laksmanjoo's Shiva Sutras

"The Five Agreements are tools to change your world. If you are impeccable with your word, if you don't take anything personally, if you don't make assumptions, if you always do your best, and if you are skeptical while listening, there won't be any more war in your head, there will be peace." – Don Miguel Ruiz

THE FIVE AGREEMENTS

BE IMPECCABLE WITH YOUR WORD

Speak with integrity. Say only what you mean. Avoid using the word to speak against yourself or to gossip about others. Use the power of your word in the direction of truth and love.

DON'T TAKE ANYTHING PERSONALLY

Nothing others do is because of you. What others say and do is a projection of their own reality, their own dream. When you are immune to the opinions and actions of others, you won't be the victim of needless suffering.

DON'T MAKE ASSUMPTIONS

Find the courage to ask questions and to express what you really want. Communicate with others as clearly as you can to avoid misunderstandings, sadness, and drama. With just this one agreement, you can completely transform your life.

ALWAYS DO YOUR BEST

Your best is going to change from moment to moment; it will be different when you are healthy as opposed to sick. Under any circumstances, simply do your best, and you will avoid self-judgement, self-abuse, and regret.

BE SKEPTICAL, BUT LEARN TO LISTEN

Don't believe yourself or anybody else. Use the power of doubt to question everything you hear: Is it really the truth? Listen to the intent behind words, and you will understand the real message.

Source: The Fifth Agreements by Don Miguel Ruiz and Don Jose Ruiz, 2010.

Buddha Quotations

The word "Buddha" means "Awakened one" or "Enlightened one" in Sanskrit and Pali.

These Buddha quotations – sacred sutras – are enlightening quotations that have a very deep meaning. They are perfect to use as a meditation focus, and to reflect upon ways in how you live your own life.

Siddhartha Gautama (563 BCE to 483 BCE), the Buddha, was the awakened or enlightened spiritual teacher who founded Buddhism.

Most of His teachings had to do with ethics and correct understanding of how life should be lived such as "Nothing is permanent," "What we think, we become," "There is no way to happiness, happiness is the way," and the following selected quotations:

"I teach one thing and one thing only: that is, suffering and the end of suffering."

"Have compassion for all beings, rich and poor alike; each has their suffering. Some suffer too much, others too little."

"The cause of all pain and suffering is ignorance."

"Pain is inevitable. Suffering is optional."

"Hate is never conquered by hate. Hate is only conquered by love."

"The secret of health for both mind and body is not to mourn for the past, nor to worry about the future, or not to anticipate troubles, but to live the present moment wisely and earnestly."

"To enjoy good health, to bring true happiness to one's family, to bring peace to all, one must first discipline and control one's own mind. If a man can control his mind he can find the way to Enlightenment, and all wisdom and virtue will naturally come to him."

"To keep the body in good health is a duty... otherwise we shall not be able to keep our mind strong and clear."

"Your body is precious. It is our vehicle for awakening. Treat it with care."

"Without health life is not life; it is only a state of languor and suffering – an image of death."

"Health is the greatest gift, contentment the greatest wealth, faithfulness the best relationship."

"Hunger (for things) is the supreme disease."

"The mind is everything. What you think you become."

"All wrong-doing arises because of mind. If mind is transformed can wrong-doing remain?"

"We are what we think. All that we are arises with our thoughts. With our thoughts, we make the world."

"It is a man's own mind, not his enemy or foe, that lures him to evil ways."

"The tongue like a sharp knife... Kills without drawing blood."

"Holding on to anger is like grasping a hot coal with the intent of throwing it at someone else; you are the one who gets burned."

"We are formed and molded by our thoughts. Those whose minds are shaped by selfless thoughts give joy when they speak or act. Joy follows them like a shadow that never leaves them."

"Whatever words we utter should be chosen with care for people will hear them and be influenced by them for good or ill."

"Better than a thousand hollow words, is one word that brings peace."

"The thought manifests as the word. The word manifests as the deed. The deed develops into habit. And the habit hardens into character. So watch the thought and its ways with care. And let it spring from love, born out of concern for all beings."

"The wise ones fashioned speech with their thought, sifting it as grain is sifted through a sieve."

"However many holy words you read, however many you speak, what good will they do you if you do not act on upon them?"

"I never see what has been done; I only see what remains to be done."

"To be idle is a short road to death and to be diligent is a way of life; foolish people are idle, wise people are diligent."

"An idea that is developed and put into action is more important than an idea that exists only as an idea."

"Believe nothing, no matter where you read it, or who said it, no matter if I have said it, unless it agrees with your own reason and your own common sense."

"An insincere and evil friend is more to be feared than a wild beast; a wild beast may wound your body, but an evil friend will wound your mind."

"There has to be evil so that good can prove its purity above it." "Virtue

is persecuted more by the wicked than it is loved by the good."

"When one has the feeling of dislike for evil, when one feels tranquil, one finds pleasure in listening to good teachings; when one has these feelings and appreciate them, one is free of fear."

"The whole secret of existence is to have no fear. Never fear what will become of you, depend on no one. Only the moment you reject all help are you freed."

"Even death is not to be feared by one who has lived wisely."

"You can search the entire universe for someone who is more deserving of your love and affection than you are yourself, and that person is not to be found anywhere. You yourself, as much as anybody in the entire universe deserve your love and affection."

"Just as a candle cannot burn without fire, men cannot live without a spiritual life."

"Peace comes from within. Do not seek it without."

"Those who are free of resentful thoughts surely find peace."

"To live a pure unselfish life, one must count nothing as one's own in the midst of abundance."

"There are only two mistakes one can make along the road to truth, not going all the way, and not starting."

"Three things cannot be long hidden: the sun, the moon, and the truth."

"No one saves us but ourselves. No one can and no one may. We ourselves must walk the path."

"Work out your own salvation. Do not depend on others."

"To conquer oneself is a greater task than conquering others."

"The only real failure in life is not to be true to the best one knows."

"Your work is to discover your work and then with all your heart to give yourself to it."

"Thousands of candles can be lighted from a single candle, and the life of the candle will not be shortened. Happiness never decreases by being shared."

"Meditation brings wisdom; lack of meditation leaves ignorance. Know well what leads you forward and what hold you back, and choose the path that leads to wisdom."

"We live in illusion and appearance of things. There is reality. We are that reality. When you understand this, you see that you are nothing, and being nothing, you are everything. That is all."

"Silence is an empty space, space is the home of the awakened mind."

"The way is not in the sky. The way is in the heart."

"To understand everything is to forgive everything."

"Do not dwell in the past, do not dream of the future, concentrate the mind on the present moment."

"Life can only take place in the present moment. If we lose the present moment, we lose life."

"There is only one moment in time when it is necessary to awaken. That moment is now."

"Awake. Be the witness of your thoughts. You are what observes, not what you observe."

"You cannot travel the path until you have become the path itself."

"He who experiences the unity of life sees his own self in all beings and all beings in his own self and looks on everything with an impartial eye."

"There have been many Buddhas before me and will be many Buddhas in the future."

"All living beings have the Buddha nature and can become Buddhas."

Can You Hear the Mountain Stream?

A Zen Master was walking in silence with one of his disciples along a mountain trail. When they came to an ancient cedar tree, they sat down under it for a simple meal of some rice and vegetables. After the meal, the disciple, a young monk who had not yet found the key to the mystery of Zen, broke the silence by asking the Master, "Master, how do I enter Zen?"

He was, of course, inquiring how to enter the state of consciousness which is Zen.

The Master remained silent. Almost five minutes passed while the disciple anxiously waited for an answer. He was about to ask another question when the Master suddenly spoke, "Do you hear the sound of that mountain stream?"

The disciple had not been aware of any mountain stream. He had been too busy thinking about the meaning of Zen. Now, as he began to listen for the sound, his noisy mind subsided. At first he heard nothing. Then, his thinking gave way to heightened alertness, and suddenly he did hear the hardly perceptible murmur of a small stream in the far distance.

"Yes, I can hear it now," he said.

The Master raised his finger and, with a look in his eyes that in some way was both fierce and gentle, said, "Enter Zen from there."

The disciple was stunned. It was his first satori – a flash of enlightenment. He knew what Zen was without knowing what it was that he knew!

They continued on their journey in silence. The disciple was amazed at the aliveness of the world around him. He experienced everything as if for the first time. Gradually, however, he started thinking again. The alert stillness became covered up again by mental noise, and before long he had another question. "Master, he said, "I have been thinking. What would you have said if I hadn't been able to hear the mountain stream?" The Master stopped, looked at him, raised his finger and said, "Enter Zen from there."

Good and Bad

The deeper interconnectedness of all things and events implies that the mental labels of "good" and "bad" are ultimately illusory. They always imply a limited perspective and so are true only relatively and temporarily. This is illustrated in the story of a wise man who won an expensive car in a lottery. His family and friends were very happy for him and came to celebrate. "Isn't it great!" they said. "You are so lucky." The man smiled and said, "Maybe." For a few weeks he enjoyed driving his car. Then one day a drunken driver crashed into his new car at an intersection and he ended up in the hospital, with multiple injuries. His family and friends came to see him and said, "That was really unfortunate." Again the man smiled and said, "Maybe." While he was still in the hospital, one night there was a landslide and his house fell into the sea. Again his friends came the next day and said, "Weren't you lucky to have been here in hospital." Again he said, "Maybe."

The wise man's "maybe" signifies a refusal to judge anything that happens. Instead of judging what is, he accepts it and enters into conscious alignment with the higher order. He knows that often it is impossible for the mind to understand what place or purpose a seemingly random event has in the tapestry of the whole. But there are no random events, nor are there events or things that exist by and for themselves, in isolation. The atoms that make up your body were once forged inside stars, and the causes of even the smallest event are virtually infinite and connected with the whole in incomprehensible ways. If you wanted to trace back the cause of any event, you would have to go back all the way to the beginning of creation. The cosmos is not chaotic. The very word cosmos means order. But this is not an order the human mind can ever comprehend, although it can sometimes glimpse it.

Is That So?

The Zen Master Hakuin lived in a town in Japan. He was held in high regard and many people came to him for spiritual teaching. Then it happened that the teenage daughter of his next-door neighbor became pregnant. When being questioned by her angry and scolding parents as to the identity of the father, she finally told them that he was Hakuin, the Zen Master. In great anger the parents rushed to Hakuin and told him with much shouting and accusing that their daughter had confessed that he was the father. All he replied was, "Is that so?"

News of the scandal spread throughout the town and beyond. The master lost his reputation. This did not trouble him. Nobody came to see him anymore. He remained unmoved. When the child was born, the parents brought the baby to Hakuin. "You are the father, so you look after him." The Master took loving care of the child. A year later, the mother remorsefully confessed to her parents that the real father of the child was the young man who worked at the butcher shop. In great distress they went to see Hakuin to apologize and ask for forgiveness. "We are really sorry. We have come to take the baby back. Our daughter confessed that you are not the father." "Is that so?" is all he would say as he handed the baby over to them.

The Master responds to falsehood and truth, bad news and good news, in exactly the same way: "Is that so?" He allows the form of the moment, good or bad, to be as it is and so does not become a participant in human drama. To him there is only this moment, and this moment is as it is. Events are not personalized. He is nobody's victim. He is so completely at one with what happens that what happens has no power over him anymore. Only if you resist what happens are you at the mercy of what happens, and the world will determine your happiness and unhappiness.

The baby is looked after with loving care. Bad turns into good through the power of nonresistance. Always responding to what what the present moment requires, he lets go of the baby when it is time to do so.

Imagine briefly how the ego would have reacted during the various stages of the unfolding of these events.

This, too, will pass

According to an ancient Sufi story, there lived a king in some Middle Eastern land who was continuously torn between happiness and despondency. The slightest thing would cause him great upset or provoke an intense reaction, and his happiness would quickly turn into disappointment and despair. A time came when the king finally got tired of himself and of life, and he began to seek a way out. He sent for a wise man who lived in his kingdom and who was reputed to be enlightened. When the wise man came, the king said to him, "I want to be like you. Can you give me something that will bring balance, serenity, and wisdom into my life? I will pay any price you ask."

The wise man said, "I may be able to help you. But the price is so great that your entire kingdom would not be sufficient payment for it. Therefore it will be a gift for you if you will honor it." The king gave his assurance, and the wise man left.

A few weeks later, he returned and handed the king an ornate box carved in jade. The king opened the box and found a simple gold ring inside. Some letters were inscribed on the ring. The inscription read: This, too, will pass. "What is the meaning of this?" asked the king. The wise man said, "Wear this ring always. Whatever happens, before you call it good or bad, touch this ring and read the inscription. That way, you will always be at peace."

This, too, will pass. What is about these simple words that makes them so powerful? Looking at it superficially, it would seem while those words may provide some comfort in a bad situation, they would also diminish the enjoyment of the good things in life. "Don't be too happy, because it won't last." This seems to be what they are saying when applied in a situation that is perceived as good.

The full import of these words becomes clear when we consider them in the context of two other stories that we encountered earlier. The story of the Zen Master whose only response was always "Is that so?" shows the good that comes through inner nonresistance to events, that is to say, being at one with what happens. The story of the man whose comment was invariably a laconic "Maybe" illustrates the wisdom of nonjudgement, and the story of the ring points to the fact of impermanence which, when recognized, leads to nonattachment. Nonresistance, nonjudgement, and nonattachment are the three aspects of true freedom and enlightened living.

Conclusion

"Where awareness (attention) goes, energy flows
Where energy flows, awareness follows."

Going with the flow of Qi and being in the flow is expressed in the Qigong principle Yi Dao Qi Dao – "where awareness (or attention) goes, energy flows" – and Qi Dao Yi Dao – "where energy flows, awareness follows."

The above Qigong principle Qi Dao Yi Dao – "where energy flows, awareness follows" taught us simply to put our awareness (attention) in the now or present rather then the past or the future in order to experience joy, peace and oneness with your true Self, Being or Divine Presence. With the regular practice in putting our awareness (attention) in the now, we will become conscious of an awareness of Being or Presence that is beyond the mind characterized with quieting of the mind, peace and joy.

According to Eckhart Tolle's How to Experience Total Freedom, "Access the power of Now. That is the key. The power of Now is none other than the power of your presence, your consciousness liberated from thought forms. So deal with the past on the level of the present. The more attention you give to the past, the more you energize it, and the more likely you are to make a "self" out of it.

Don't misunderstand: Attention is essential, but not to the past as past. Give attention to the present; give attention to your behavior, to your reactions, moods, thoughts, emotions, fears, and desires as they occur in the present. There's the past in you. If you can be present enough to watch all those things, not critically or analytically but nonjudgmentally, then you are dealing with the past and dissolving it through the power of your presence.

You cannot find yourself by going into the past. You find yourself by coming into the present."

There are other portals for spiritual empowerment that can be used to access the Unmanifested Source other than being intensely present, and these are: getting in touch with the energy field of your lightbody, disidentify from the mind, surrender to what is, paying attention in the gap between sound and silence, and the gap between object and space, and paying attention in the gap between inbreath and outbreath.

According to Eckhart Tolle, "Every portal is a portal of death, the death of the false self. When you go through it, you cease to derive your identity from your psychological, mind-made form. You then realize that death is an illusion, just as identification with form was an illusion. The end of illusion – that's all that death is. It is painful only as long as you cling to illusion."

"In the Sermon on the Mount, Jesus makes a prediction that to this day few people have understood. He says, "Blessed are the meek, for they shall inherit the earth." In the modern versions of the Bible, "meek" is translated as humble. Who are the meek or the humble, and what does it mean that they shall inherit the earth?

The meek are the egoless. They are those who have awakened to their essential true nature as consciousness and recognize that essence in all "others," all life-forms. They live in the surrendered state and so feel their oneness with the whole and the Source. They embody the awakened consciousness that is changing all aspects of life on our planet, including nature, because life on earth is inseparable from the human consciousness that perceives and interacts with it. That is the sense in which the meek will inherit the earth."

May you practice the Omkabah Lightbody Activation meditation with Maitreya (Shiva) Shen Gong covered in the accompanying videos to further quiet your mind, master awareness, transformation and intent, develop your energy bubble (lightbody) or energy field, cultivate your Three Treasures – Jing, Qi and Shen – and open your heart to unconditional love, the essence of your true Self. Without developing your kinesthetic awareness – awareness of movement through Qigong – you cannot experience life fully with a greater sense of well-being and spiritual awakening, simply because all life is movement.

Because the awakening experience is present in silence and stillness, surrender and acceptance to what is, and is beyond thoughts that cannot be known through words – which can only serve as pointers to truth only – personal one-on-one contact and facilitation by the awakened presence of an enlightened teacher through his words, look or touch is the fastest way to have a first-hand experience in spiritual awakening, personal transformation and freedom.

May the grace of God, Being or Presence bestow on you an awakening through mastery of awareness – the space in which thoughts exist when that space has become conscious of itself.

Inner peace, love, blissful joy, creativity, strengthening of my immune system, slowing down of the aging process, speedy healing of diseases and addictions, and overall health improvement have been the added benefits from the continuous spiritual awakening through the mastery of awareness by the regular practice of meditation and Qigong – meditation on the gap, breath awareness, acceptance and surrender to what is, being intensely present, disidentify from the mind, and getting in touch with the energy field of the inner body with physical body movement – finding balance and recognition as a human being, between human form and formless Being.

However, you must meditate regularly and persistently, to strengthen your self-awareness. Along the way, you may have many kinds of experiences, but the ultimate state is beyond all experiences. In the Self-realized state there is only bliss. True meditation is to become immersed there.

"We are what we think. All that we are arises with our thoughts. With our thoughts, we make the world."

"You can search the entire universe for someone who is more deserving of your love and affection than you are yourself, and that person is not to be found anywhere. You yourself, as much as anybody in the entire universe deserve your love and affection."

"There is no way to happiness, happiness is the way."

"Peace comes from within. Do not seek it without."

"Your work is to discover your work and then with all your heart to give yourself to it."

"Silence is an empty space, space is the home of the awakened mind." – Siddhartha Gautama Buddha

Meditation is a simple and direct means to experience within you an inner stillness – an inner space or awareness – an ocean of love, peace, joy, happiness and well-being in a continuous basis.

"Awake. Be the witness of your thoughts. You are what observes, not what you observe."

"There have been many Buddhas before me and will be many Buddhas in the future."

"All living beings have the Buddha nature and can become Buddhas." – Siddhartha Gautama Buddha

"Through awareness, emotions and even thoughts become depersonalized. Their impersonal nature is recognized. There is no longer a self in them. They are just human emotions, human thoughts. Your entire personal history, which is ultimately no more than a story, a bundle of thoughts and emotions, becomes of secondary importance and no longer occupies the forefront of your consciousness. It no longer forms the basis for your sense of identity. You are the light of Presence, the awareness that is prior to and deeper than any thoughts and emotions." – Eckhart Tolle

"The dancer in this field of universal dance is his Self of universal consciousness." 10 – Shiva Sutra 3.9

"Ignorance is the root cause of all suffering. It is also the forgetfulness of one's own Self." – Shankaracharya, Aparokshanubhuti, 17

"Moksa or liberation is nothing else but the awareness of one's true nature." – Abhinavagupta, Tantra I, p. 192

"Neither reject anything, nor accept, abide in your essential Self which is an Eternal presence." Abhinavagupta, Anuttarastika, 2

"One's own thoughts is one's world. What a person thinks is what he becomes – that is the eternal mystery. If the mind dwells within the supreme Self, One enjoys undying happiness." – Maitri Upanishad

When you lose yourself in the world, you forget your rootedness in Being, your divine reality. Confusion, anger, depression, violence, and conflict arise when humans forget who they are. Ignorance of our true nature is the root cause of all pain and suffering. It is also the forgetfulness of one's own Self. That is why Buddha said:

"To enjoy good health, to bring true happiness to one's family, to bring peace to all, one must first discipline and control one's own mind. If a man can control his mind he can find the way to Enlightenment, and all wisdom and virtue will naturally come to him."

"Awake. Be the witness of your thoughts. You are what observes, not what you observe."

"The cause of all pain and suffering is ignorance."

"Pain is inevitable. Suffering is optional."

Yet how easy it is to remember the truth and thus return home:

> I am not my thoughts, emotions, senses,
> perceptions, and experiences.
> I am not the content of my life.
> I am Life.
> I am the space in which all things happen.
> I am consciousness.
> I am the Now.
> I Am that I Am.

IMPORTANT NOTE ON HOLOGRAPHIC SOUND HEALING

HOLOGRAPHIC SOUND HEALING on page 136: Holographic Sound Healing together with Maitreya (Shiva) Shen Gong and Omkabah Heart Lightbody Activation will completely and exponentially amplify the vibration of sound and light body for healing, balancing, body rejuvenation, interdimensional travel, manifestation, ascension and much, much more as I have experienced it in my regular practice and clinical healing application

References & Recommended Books:

Play of Consciousness by Swami Muktananda, 1978.

VijnanaBhairava or Divine Consciousness by J Singh, 1979

Where Are You Going? by Swami Muktananda, 1981.

Five Elements and Ten Stems by Kiiko Matsumoto and Stephen Birch, 1983.

Hara Diagnosis: Reflections on the Sea by Kiiko Matsumoto & Stephen Birch, 1988.

Secrets of Mayan Science and Religion by Hunbatz Men, 1989.

The Yellow Emperor's Classic of Medicine by Maoshing Ni, 1995.

Radiant Health, the Ancient Wisdom of the Chinese Tonic Herbs by Ron Teeguarden, 1998.

Pan Gu Mystical Qigong by Ou Wen Wei, 1999.

Meditations for Soul Realization by Choa Kok Sui, 2000.

Practicing the Power the Now by Eckhart Tolle, 2001.

Tao of Life: An Investigation of Sundo Taoism's Personal Growth Model as a Process of Spiritual Development by Hyunmoon Kim, 2002.

Stillness Speaks by Eckhart Tolle, 2003.

Sheng Zhen Wuji Yuan Gong, A Return to Oneness by Li Jun Feng, 2004.

Hara: The Vital Center of Man by Karlfried Graf Durckheim, 2004.

The Power of Now, A Guide to Spiritual Enlightenment, by Eckhart Tolle, 2004.

A New Earth, Awakening to Your Life's Purpose, by Eckhart Tolle, 2005.

Chinese Medical Qigong Therapy. vol 1. Pacific Grove: The International Institute of Medical Qigong, 2005. 211-33. Print, Jerry Alan Johnson

Eckhart Tolle's Findhorn Retreat, Stillness Amidst the World, 2006.

Empty Force: The Power of Chi for Self-Defense and Energy Healing by Paul Dong, 2006.

The Existence of God is Self-Evident by Choa Kok Sui, 2006.

Kashmir Shaivism the Secret Supreme by Swami Lakshmanjoo, 2007.

Shiva Sutras, the Supreme Awakening by Swami Lakshmanjoo, 2007.

Qi Dao – Tibetan Shamanic Qigong by Lama Tantrapa, 2007.

Serpent of Light: Beyond 2012 by Drunvalo Melchizedek, 2008.

Universal Love, The Yoga Method of Buddha Maitreya by Lama Yeshe, 2008.

Oneness with All Life: Inspirational Selections from A New Earth by Eckhart Tolle, 2009.

The Fifth Agreement, A Practical Guide to Self-Mastery, by don Miguel Ruiz & don Jose Ruiz, 2010.

Glossary of Terms

ABHINAVAGUPTA lived in Kashmir about the end of the tenth and beginning of eleventh centuries (924-1020 CE). * A versatile genius he injected new meaning into Shaiva Philosophy.

As an original thinker he shattered to pieces the established belief which laid heavy emphasis on caste and gender restrictions in relation to spiritual practice. He took to task those philosophical systems which held the prerequisite that spirituality required rigorous discipline—systems which made the quest for enlightenment the legitimate right of a chosen few. He abhorred the idea that spiritual revelation was only possible in a purely monastic surrounding, or that those caught in the householder way of life had to wait till the last portion of life before they could fully give themselves to spiritual pursuits. This idea was best expressed by Abhinavagupta in one of his concluding verses of Patanjali's Paramarthasara:

"O MY DEVOTEES! ON THIS PATH OF SUPREME BHAIRAVA, WHOEVER HAS TAKEN A STEP WITH PURE DESIRE, NO MATTER IF THAT DESIRE IS SLOW OR INTENSE; IT DOES NOT MATTER IF HE IS A BRAHMIN, IF HE IS A SWEEPER, IF HE IS AN OUTCAST, OR IF HE IS ANYBODY; HE BECOMES ONE WITH PARA-BHAIRAVA." (103)

Abhinavagupta's ideas were radical for his time, but since he spoke from the level of direct experience no one was capable of refuting him.
Having achieved the eight great *siddhi* powers he clearly exhibited the six illustrious spiritual signs of *Rudra Shakti samavesha*: unswerving devotional attachment to Shiva; full attainment of *mantra siddhi;* control over the five elements; capacity to accomplish any desired end; complete mastery over the science of rhetoric and poetry; and the spontaneous dawning of knowledge of all philosophies.

Baihui -- acupoint located at the top of the head, the center of the crown.

consciousness -- state of awareness.

Consciousness -- the intelligent, pure, supreme energy that pervades all.

Dantian -- the storage place of qi in the body, about two inches below the navel.

Enlightenment -- the state of full realization of being one with all, with God.

Gong -- effort, exertion.

Kundalini is Sanskrit for "snake" or "serpent power," so-called because it is believed to lie like a serpent in the root chakra at the base of the spine. In Tantra Yoga kundalini is an aspect of Shakti, the divine female energy and consort of Shiva. The Sahasrara or crown chakra is often called the abode of Shiva. It is also the goal of Kundalini when, as Shakti, she rises to reunite with Shiva. In Tantric Yoga the Brahman Self is attained through the reunion of Shiva and Shakti in the Sahasrara. Mother earth's kundalini is called serpent of light or great white snake strongly present in sacred sites.

Laogong -- the acupoint located at the center of the palms.

Lotus -- flower symbolic of enlightenment and purity; refers to a sitting position used in yoga.

Meditation -- a method or practice to awaken consciousness.

Merkaba (lightbody) is an interdimensional counterclockwise rotational vehicle of Light, Pranic or energy body and Soul.

Ni-wuan -- the point located in the head at the intersection between the center of the eyebrows (yin-tang) and the top of the head (baihui).

Qi -- vital energy or life force.

Qigong -- the principle of the continuous interchange of qi with qi as in that between man and the universe; the form or practice of activity engaging in this continuous interchange; the state of merging, being in the flow as in a meditative state.

Shaktipat: literally, the "descent of grace." The transmission of spiritual power (Shakti) from Guru to disciple, awakening the disciple's dormant spiritual energy, Kundalini.

Sheng Zhen -- unconditional, pure love; most sacred, highest truth. Three Treasures – Jing (essence), Qi (vitality) and Shen (Spirit).

Toltec is a Nahuatl word meaning artist. A Toltec is an artist of the spirit, and as artists we like beauty; we don't like what is not beauty. If we become better artists, our virtual reality becomes a better reflection of the truth, and we can create a masterpiece of heaven with our art.

Wuji -- before the beginning of time before the duality of yin and yang.

Xing -- character; the growth that comes from experiencing and knowing nature; enlightened consciousness.

Xiuxing -- contemplating, striving, and working towards enlightenment; the act of walking a path to enlightenment by applying what one has learned from self-inquiry and contemplation.

Yi qi -- primordial, first qi.

Yin-tang -- acupoint located at the center of the eyebrows. Yongquan -- acupoint located at the center of the soles of the feet. Yuan -- primordial, original.

Zhong mai -- the principal channel in the center of the body which connects the dantian to the niwuan - the dantian being earth and the niwuan being Heaven.

Zhongtian -- to flow through freely - to be able to pass free of obstacles within oneself and others, to arrive at Oneness.

FLOWER OF LIFE

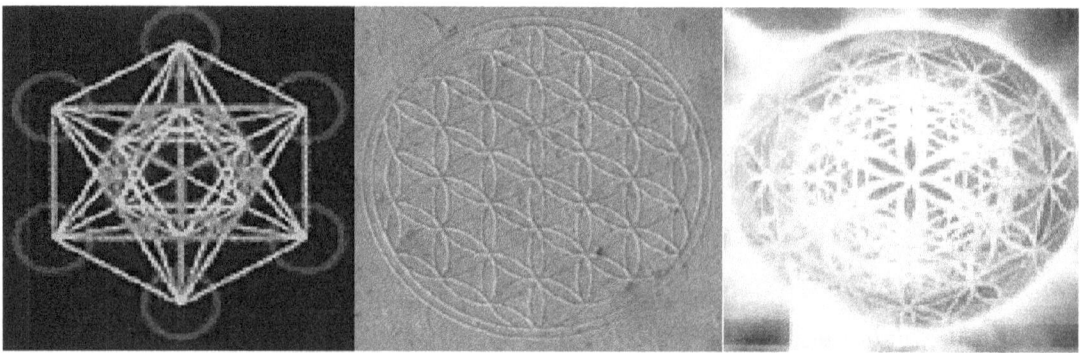

The Flower of Life holds a secret symbol created by drawing 13 circles out of the Flower of Life. By doing this, one can discover the most important and sacred pattern in the universe.

The most common form of the "Flower of Life" is hexagonal pattern (where the center of each circle is on the circumference of six surrounding circles of the same diameter), made up of 19 complete circles and 36 partial circular arcs, enclosed by a large circle.

The "Seed of Life" is formed from seven circles being placed with six fold symmetry, forming a pattern of circles and lenses, which acts as a basic component of the Flower of Life's design.

The "Flower of Life" can be found in all major religions of the world. It contains the patterns of creation as they emerged from the "Great Void". Everything is made from the Creator's thought. This same structure as it is further developed, creates the human body and all of the energy systems including the ones used to create the Merkaba. All sacred geometrical shapes are within the Flower of Life.

The complete flower also contains the three dimensional "Metatron Cube", which holds all the Platonic solids. Not just the building blocks of life, but the building blocks of creation itself.

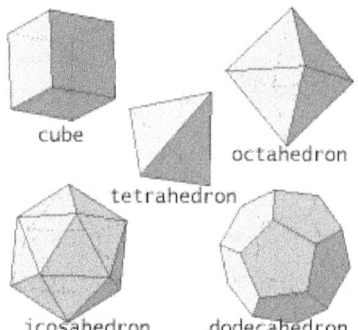

The Temple of Osiris at Abydos, Egypt contains the oldest to date example. it is carved in granite and may possibly represent the Eye of Ra a symbol of the authority of the pharaoh. Other examples can be found in Phoenician, Assyrian, Indian, Asian, Middle Eastern, and medieval art.

Sri Yantra

The Sri Yantra is the visual expression of the sound of OM. This pattern is seen by monks chanting OM. It has also been recorded electronically as a pattern which emerges during the sound of OM.

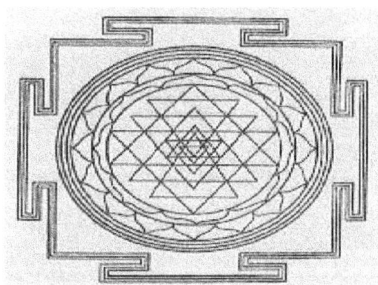

The diagram consists of nine interwoven isosceles triangles four point upwards, representing Shakti, the primordial female essence of dynamic energy, and five point downwards, representing Siva, the primordial male essence of static wisdom. It represents the goddess in her form of Shri Lalitha Or Tripura Sundari, "the beauty of the three worlds". For more info, read *Return to Oneness with Shiva* and *Oneness with Shiva*.

Credit: Sri Vidya teacher Raja Choudhury for the Shodashi mantras (maha and Trishakti) below:

Maha Shodashi Mantra (to attain liberation and material manifestation)

Om Shreem Hreem Kleem Aeem Sauh

Om Hreem Shreem

Ka E I La Hreem

Ha Sa Ka Ha La Hreem

Sa Ka La Hreem

Sauh Aeem Kleem Hreem Shreem Namah

Om
Aeem Hreem Shreem Kleem Vadavada Vagvadini Aeem Sauh Hamsah
Aam Hreem Krom Kleem Shreem Hum Swaha

OM mantra spoken

Quotations on the mantra OM

In the beginning was the Word,
and the Word was with God,
and the Word was God. - John 1:1

In the beginning was Brahman, with whom was the Word;
and the Word was truly the Supreme Brahman. - Rig Veda

The Word of Isvara (God) is AUM or OM. - Yoga Sutras of Patanjali Book 1:27

The Eternal Word - OM
by Swami Omkarananda

OM is essentially mystic, and therefore, wholly non-sectarian. The people of all religious denominations, and particularly the seekers after the divine Truth, have always, through the millenniums, used this word of divine Nature and Power, with immense spiritual profit.

The mystic seers of the ancient times received many revelations on the sacrosanct form and the ontological implications of the character of OM. They conducted prolonged experiments in its vibrations, and made many researches in the spiritual effects it exerts, the diversity of utility it permits, and the benefits it confers.

Quotes on the Mantra OM
By Master Choa Kok Sui

How do you achieve inner stillness? You do not achieve stillness by stopping the thinking process, but by being aware of the inner stillness. Where is this inner stillness located? It is in the "gap". The mantra OM helps, but it is not enough. What is more important is being aware of the interval between two OMs. Between two OMs, there is a gap or stillness. This is called Meditation on the Gap.

The mantra OM or AUM has a purifying effect and helps the consciousness shift to a higher level. The mantra OM or AUM is not only practiced by the Indians, Tibetans and the Chinese, but also by Kabbalists.

By regularly chanting the Om or AUM, it is possible to purify the incarnated soul, thereby resulting in union with the higher soul. One could also use OM to purify an object, or a certain place or area. If a person suffers from psychological pain or hurt, or some other (emotional) problems such as hatred or anger or criticizing other people, the regular chanting of OM or Amen may help over a long period of time.

The OM is a universal sound similar to Aum or Amen. Its purpose is to blend ones individual consciousness with Divine consciousness. Powerful energies emitted by OM can be used to disintegrate diseased and negative energies in the meditator as well as the environment. It cleanses, energizes, removes stress, elevates Consciousness, and creates an energetically Clean, Peaceful & Spiritual Environment.

By regularly listening to the chanting of the mantra OM by the spiritual teacher, it is possible to purify the incarnated Soul (lower Self), thereby resulting in union with the Higher Soul (Higher Self).

The aura, chakras and the different subtle bodies are further purified, by chanting the mantra OM.

Also, by chanting the mantra OM, the consciousness of the soul is raised to a higher frequency, thereby eventually enabling it to function in the higher world.

By meditating on the stillness between two OMs. Through stillness, the soul is able to function in the higher inner world.

The mantra OM or AUM, the creative Word, is connected with the sound of creation. When a person meditates deeply, the inner OM or AUM can be heard.

"The Inner Sound is continuously used in the process of creation. Therefore, creation is a continuous process. In some religious texts the Sound is called the Word.

The Sound or the Word is used as a mass noun. Creation implies differentiation; therefore, there are many Sounds or Words that are continuously used in the process of creation." - Sutra 18 from The Existence of God is Self-Evident

Mantra of Compassion OM MANI PADME HUM

The Mantra of Compassion, OM MANI PADME HUM, is pronounced by Tibetans: Om Mani Peme Hung. It embodies the compassion and blessing of all the buddhas and bodhisattvas, and invokes especially the blessing of Avalokiteshvara, the Buddha of Compassion. Avalokiteshvara is a manifestation of the Buddha in the Sambhogakaya, and his mantra is considered the essence of the Buddha's compassion for all beings. Just as Padmasambhava is the most important master for the Tibetan people, Avalokiteshvara is their most important buddha, and karmic deity of Tibet. There is a famous saying that the Buddha of Compassion became so embedded in the Tibetan consciousness that any child who could say the word "mother" could also recite the mantra OM MANI PADME HUM.

Countless ages ago, it is said, a thousand princes vowed to become buddhas. One resolved to become the Buddha we know as Gautama Siddharta; Avalokiteshvara, however, vowed not to attain enlightenment until all the other thousand princes had themselves become buddhas. In his infinite compassion, he vowed too to liberate all sentient beings from the suffering of the different realms of samsara. Before the buddhas of the ten directions, he prayed: "May I help all beings, and if ever I tire in this great work, may my body be shattered into a thousand pieces." First, it is said, he descended into the hell realms, ascending gradually through the world of hungry ghosts, up to the realm of the gods. From there he happened to look down and saw, aghast, that though he had saved innumerable beings from hell, countless more were pouring in. This plunged him into the profoundest grief; for a moment he almost lost faith in that noble vow he had taken, and his body exploded into a thousand pieces. In his desperation, he called out to all the buddhas for help, who came to his aid from all directions of the universe, as one text said, like a soft blizzard of snowflakes. With their great power the buddhas made him whole again, and from then on Avalokisteshvara had eleven heads, and a thousand arms, and on each palm of each palm of each hand was an eye, signifying that union of wisdom and skillful means that is the mark of true compassion. In this form he was even more resplendent and empowered than before to help all beings, and his compassion grew even more intense as again and again he repeated this vow before the buddhas: "May I not attain final buddhahood before all sentient beings attain enlightenment."

It is said that in his sorrow at the pain of samsara, two tears fell from his eyes: through the blessings of the buddhas, they were transformed into two Taras. One is Tara in her green form, who is the active force of compassion, and the other is Tara in her white form, who is compassion's motherly aspect. The name Tara means "she who liberates": she who ferries us across the ocean of samsara.

In the words of the poem:
Avalokiteshvara is like the moon
Whose cool light puts out the burning fires of samsara
In its rays the night-flowering lotus of compassion
Opens wide its petals.

The teachings explain that each of the six syllables of the mantra -- OM MANI PADME HUM -- has a specific and potent effect in bringing about transformation at different levels of our being. The six syllables purify completely the six poisonous negative emotions, which are the manifestation of ignorance, and which cause us to act negatively with our body, speech and mind, so creating samsara and our suffering in it. Pride, jealousy, desire, ignorance, greed, and anger are transformed, through the mantra, into their true nature, the wisdoms of the six buddha families that become manifest in the enlightened mind.

So when we recite OM MANI PADME HUM, the six negative emotions, which are the cause of the six realms of samsara, are purified. This is how reciting the six syllables prevents rebirth in each of the six realms, and also dispels the suffering inherent in each realm. At the same time reciting OM MANI PADME HUM completely purifies the aggregates of ego, the skandhas, and perfects the six kinds of transcendental action of the heart of the enlightened mind, the paramitas of: generosity, harmonious conduct, endurance, enthusiasm, concentration, and insight. It is also said that OM MANI PADME HUM grants strong protection from all kinds of negative influences, and various different forms of illness.

Often HRIH, the "seed syllable" of Avalokiteshvara, is added to the mantra to make OM MANI PADME HUM HRIH. The essence of the compassion of the Buddhas, HRIH, is the catalyst that activates the compassion of the Buddhas to transform our negative emotions into their wisdom nature.

Kalu Rinpoche writes:

Another way of interpreting the mantra is that the syllable OM is the essence of enlightened form; MANI PADME, the four syllables in the middle, represent the speech of enligtenment; and the last syllable, HUM, represents the mind of enlightenment. The body, speech, and mind of all the buddhas and bodhisattvas are inherent in the sound of the mantra. It purifies the obscurations of body, speech, and mind, and brings all beings to the state of realization. When it is joined with our own faith and efforts in meditation and recitation, the transformative power of the mantra arises and develops. It is truly possible to purify ourselves in this way.

For those who are familiar with the mantra and have recited it with fervor and faith all their lives, the Tibetan Book of the Dead prays that in the bardo: "When the sound of dharmata roars like a thousand thunders, may it all become the sound of the six-syllables." Similarly we read in the Surangama Sutra:

How sweetly mysterious is the transcendental sound of Avalokiteshvara. It is the primordial sound of the universe ... It is the subdued murmur of the sea-tide setting inward. Its mysterious sound brings liberation and peace to all sentient beings who in their pain are calling out for help, and it brings a sense of serene stability to all those who are seeking Nirvana's boundless peace.

OM AH HUM VAJRA GURU PADMA SIDDHI HUM

The Vajra Guru mantra, OM AH HUM VAJRA GURU PADMA SIDDHI HUM, is pronounced by Tibetans: Om Ah Hung Benza Guru Pema Siddhi Hung. This explanation of its meaning is based on explanations by Dudjorn Rinpoche and Dilgo Khyentse Rinpoche.

OM AH HUM

The syllable OM AH HUM have outer, inner, and "secret" meanings. At each of these levels, however, OM stands for the body, AH for the speech, and HUM for the mind. They represent the transformative blessings of the body, speech, and mind of all the buddhas.

Externally OM purifies all the negative actions committed through your body, AH through your speech, and HUM through your mind. By purifying your body, speech, and mind, OM AH HUM grants the blessing of the body, speech, and mind of the buddhas.

OM is also the essence of the form, AH the essence of sound, and HUM the essence of mind. So by reciting this mantra, you are also purifying the environment, as well as yourself and all the other beings within it. OM purifies all perceptions, AH all sounds, and HUM the mind, its thoughts and emotions.

Internally OM purifies the subtle channels, AH the wind, inner air or flow of energy, and HUM the creative essence.

On a deeper level, OM AH HUM represent the three kayas of the Lotus family of the buddhas: OM is the Dharmakaya: the Buddha Amitabha, Buddha of Limitless Light; AH is the Sambhogakaya: Avalokiteshvara, the Buddha of Compassion; and HUM is the Nirmanakaya: Padmasambhava. This signifies, in the case of this mantra, that all three kayas are embodied in the person of Padmasambhava.

At the innermost level, OM AH HUM bring the realization of the three aspects of the nature of mind: OM brings the realization of its unceasing Energy and Compassion, AH brings the realization of its radiant nature, and HUM brings the realization of its skylike Essence

VAJRA GURU PADMA

VAJRA is compared to the diamond, the strongest and most precious of stones. Just as a diamond can cut through anything but is itself completely indestructible, so the unchanging, nondual wisdom of the buddhas can never be harmed or destroyed by ignorance, and can cut through all delusions and obscurations. The qualities and activities of the body, speech, and wisdom mind of the buddhas are able to benefit beings with the piercing, unhindered power of the diamond. And like the diamond, the Vajra is free of defects; its brilliant strength comes from the realization of the Dharmakaya nature of reality, the nature of the Buddha Amitabha.

GURU means "weighty"; someone replete with every wonderful quality, who embodies wisdom, knowledge, compassion, and skilled means. Just as gold is the weightiest and most precious of metals, so the inconceivable, flawless qualities of the Guru -- the master -- make him unsurpassable, and above all things in excellence. GURU corresponds to the Sambhogakaya, and to Avalokiteshvara, the Buddha of Compassion. Also, since Padmasambhava teaches the path of Tantra, which is symbolized by the Vajra, and through the practice of Tantra he attained supreme realization, so he is known as "the VAJRA GURU."

PADMA means lotus, and signifies the Lotus family of the buddhas, and specifically their aspect of enlightened speech. The Lotus family is the buddha family to which human beings belong. As Padmasambhava is the direct emanation, the Nirmanakaya, of Buddha Amitabha, who is the primordial buddha of the Lotus family, he is known as "PADMA." His name Padmasambhava, the "Lotus-born," in fact refers to the story of his birth on a blossoming lotus flower.

When the syllables VAJRA GURU PADMA are taken together, they also signify the essence and the blessing of the View, Meditation and Action. VAJRA means the unchanging, diamantine, indestructible Essence of the truth, which we pray to realize in our View. GURU represents the luminosity Nature and noble qualities of enlightenment, which we pray to perfect in our Meditation. PADMA stands for Compassion, which we pray to accomplish in our Action.

Through reciting the mantra, then, we receive the blessing of the wisdom mind, the noble qualities and the compassion of Padmasambhava and all the buddhas.

SIDDHI HUM

SIDDHI means "real accomplishment," "attainment," "blessing," and "realization." There are two kinds of siddhis: ordinary and supreme. Through receiving the blessing of ordinary siddhis, all obstacles in our lives, such as ill-health, are removed, all our good aspirations are fulfilled, benefits like wealth and prosperity and long life accrue to us, and all of life's various circumstances become auspicious and conducive to spiritual practice, and the realization of enlightenment.

The blessing of the supreme siddhi brings about enlightenment itself, the state of complete realization of Padmasambhava, that benefits both ourselves and all other sentient beings. So by remembering and praying to the body, speech, mind, qualities, and activity of Padmasambhava, we will come to attain both ordinary and supreme siddhis.

SIDDHI HUM is said to draw in all the siddhis like a magnet that attracts iron filings.

HUM represents the wisdom mind of the buddhas, and is the sacred catalyst of the mantra. It is like proclaiming its power and truth: "So be it!"

The essential meaning of the mantra is: "I invoke you, the Vajra Guru, Padmasambhava, by your blessing may you grant us ordinary and supreme siddhis."

Dilgo Khyentse Rinpoche explains:

It is said that the twelve syllables OM AH HUM VAJRA GURU PADMA SIDDHI HUM carry the entire blessing of the twelve types of teaching taught by the Buddha, which are the essence of his eighty-four thousand Dharmas. Therefore to recite the Vajra Guru mantra once is equivalent to the blessing of reciting ... or practicing the whole teaching of the Buddha. These twelve branches of the teachings are the antidotes to free us from the "Twelve Links of Interdependent Origination," which keep us bound to samsara: ignorance, karmic formations, discursive consciousness, name and form, senses, contact, sensation, craving, grasping, existence, birth, old age and death. These twelve links are the mechanism of samsara, by which samsara is kept alive. Through reciting the twelve syllables of the Vajra Guru mantra, these twelve links are purified, and you are able to remove and purify completely the layer of karmic emotional defilements, and so be liberated from samsara.

Although we are not able to see Padmasambhava in person, his wisdom mind has manifested in the form of the mantra; these twelve syllables are actually the emanation of his wisdom mind, and they are endowed with his entire blessing. The Vajra Guru mantra is Padmasambhava in the form of sound. So when you invoke him with the recitation of the twelve syllables, the blessing and merit you obtain is tremendous. In these difficult times, just as there is no buddha or refuge we can call upon who is more powerful than Padmasambhava, so there is no mantra that is more fitting than the Vajra Guru mantra.

ADDITIONAL NOTE by Ricardo B. Serrano, R.Ac.: White OM is focused at the forehead, Ruby red AH is focused at the throat, and sky blue HUM is focused at the heart of the practitioner while visualizing light rays radiating from Padmasambhava's forehead, throat and heart. Guru Padmasambhava is visualized above the practitioner's head.

SOURCE: The above two most famous Sanskrit Mantras in Tibet - mantra of Avalokiteshvara, the Buddha of Compassion, OM MANI PADME HUM and the mantra of Padmasambhava, called the Vajra Guru Mantra - articles are excerpts from Sogyal Rinpoche's Tibetan Book of Living and Dying, pages 393-398.

WHAT BUDDHA NATURE IS & ILLUSTRATION

A Buddhist Monk doing Advanced Spiritual Practice (Guru Yoga)
to develop the Spiritual Fetus lodged above the head

The Spiritual fetus is a symbolic term for Buddha Nature or the "incarnated Soul" that is lodged above the head. This illustration was taken from a Taoist book "Cultivating the Energy of Life" written by Liu Hua-yang and translated by Eva Wong. It is based on the book "Hui-ming ching." The text Hui-ming ching is part of the book "Wu-Liu, Hsien-Tsung" (Techniques of Immortality by Wu and Liu) by Taoist masters Wu Chung-hsiu and Liu Hua-yang.

"The Buddha Nature is lodged above the head which radiates outward, forming the aura. Through the divine cord, the three silver cords and the three permanent seeds, the different bodies (the physical body, the energy body, the astral body and the mental body) are infused with the essence of the Buddha Nature. Just as the etheric body interpenetrates the physical body, likewise the essence of the Buddha nature interpenetrates the physical body; at the same time, it is beyond the physical body. That is why the physical body is actually within the Buddha nature, and not the Buddha nature within the physical body. The physical body is like a sponge. If you put the sponge in a bathtub filled with water, the water is inside and outside the sponge. In other words, the sponge is inside the water. The physical body, energy body, astral body and lower mental body are all inside the incarnated Buddha nature. Therefore, it would be accurate to define a person as a Buddha nature with a physical body, rather than a physical body with a Buddha nature. To express this more accurately, a person is a Buddha nature with a physical body and other subtle bodies.

The Buddha nature, as seen from the point of lower clairvoyance, is spiritual energy which is fluidic in nature. But from the perspective of higher spiritual clairvoyance, the Buddha nature is radiatory and is omnipresent within a certain "radius of space." - Master Choa Kok Sui's OM MANI PADME HUM book

Guru Yoga: Merging with the Wisdom Mind of the Master

Hum!
In the northwest of the land of Oddiyana,
In the heart of a lotus flower,
Endowed with the most marvelous attainments,
You are renowned as the "Lotus-born,"
Surrounded by hosts of dakinis.
Following in your footsteps,
I pray to you: Come, inspire me with your blessing!
GURU PADMA SIDDHI HUM

O Guru Rinpoche, Precious One,
You are the embodiment of
The compassion and blessings of all the buddhas,
The only protector of beings,
My body, my possessions, my heart and soul,
Without hesitation, I surrender to you!
From now until I attain enlightenment,
In happiness or sorrow, in circumstances good or bad, in situations high or low:
I rely on you completely, O Padmasambhava, you who know me:
think of me, inspire me, guide me, make me one with you!

OM AH HUM VAJRA GURU PADMA SIDDHI HUM

I have no one else to turn to;
In these evil times, the beings of the Kaliyuga
Are sinking in a swamp of intense and unbearable suffering.
Free us from all this, O Great guru!
Grant us the four empowerments, O blessed one!
Direct your realization into our minds,
O compassionate one!
Purify our emotional and cognitive obscurations,
O powerful one!

OM AH HUM VAJRA GURU PADMA SIDDHI HUM

I pray to you from the bottom of my heart,
It's not just words or empty mouthings:
Grant your blessings from the depth of your wisdom mind,
And cause all my good aspirations to be fulfilled, I pray!

OM AH HUM VAJRA GURU PADMA SIDDHI HUM

Just as if you put your finger into water, it will get wet,
and if you put it into fire, it will burn,
so if you invest your mind in the wisdom mind of the buddhas,
it will transform into their wisdom nature.

All the buddhas, bodhisattvas, and enlightened beings are present at all moments to help us, and it is through the presence of the master that all their blessings are focused directly at us. Those who know Bodhisattva Padmasambhava know the living truth of the promise he made over a thousand years ago: "I am never far from those with faith, or even from those without it, though they do not see me. My children will always, always, be protected by my compassion."

All we need to do to receive direct help is to ask. Didn't Christ also say: "Ask, and it shall be given you: seek and ye shall find; knock and it shall be opened unto you. Everyone that asketh receiveth; and he that seeketh findeth?"

H.H. Penor Rinpoche said: "The most important qualities to ensure the success of the (Guru Yoga) practice in the students' mind are faith, devotion, trust and pure view. If a student is truly bent upon benefiting from his or her practice and his or her association with the dharma, those qualities are indispensable."

Dilgo Khyentse Rinpoche said: "There have been many incredible and incomparable masters from the noble land of India and Tibet, the Land of Snows, yet of them all, the one who has the greatest compassion and blessing toward beings in this difficult age is Padmasambhava, who embodies the compassion and wisdom of all the buddhas. One of his qualities is that he has the power to give his blessing instantly to whoever prays to him, and whatever we may pray for, he has the power to grant our wish immediately."

The Buddha says in one of the Tantras: "Of all the buddhas who have ever attained enlightenment, not a single one accomplished this without relying upon a master, and of all the thousand buddhas that will appear in this eon, none of them will attain enlightenment without relying on a master."

According to Dilgo Khyentse Rinpoche: Devotion is the essence of the path, and if we have in mind nothing but the guru and feel nothing but fervent devotion, whatever occurs is perceived as his blessing. If we simply practice with this constantly present devotion, this is prayer itself.

When all thoughts are imbued with devotion to the guru, there is a natural confidence that this will take care of whatever may happen. All forms are the guru, all sounds are prayer, and all gross and subtle thoughts arise as devotion. Everything is spontaneously liberated in the absolute nature, like knots untied in the sky.

Through the guru yoga practice, all obstacles can be removed and all blessings received. And through merging our mind with the mind of the guru and remaining in that state of inseparable union, the absolute nature will be realized. This why we should always treasure guru yoga and keep it as our foremost practice.

According to Shechen Rabjam Rinpoche: Guru Yoga should be at the heart of every practice we do. It gives our practice strength and depth, and prevents us from straying into all the side-tracks dreamed up by our wild thoughts. The very essence of Buddhist practice is to destroy ego-clinging, totally -- and the most inspiring way to do that is the through the practice of Guru Yoga.

According to Dzongsar Jamyang Khyentse Rinpoche: The purpose of Dharma practice is to attain enlightenment. Actually, attaining enlightenment is exactly the same as ridding ourselves of ignorance, and the root of ignorance is the ego. Whichever path we take, whether it's the long and disciplined route, or the short and wild one, at the end of it the essential point is that we eliminate the ego...

This is the reason why, in the Vajrayana, guru devotion, or Guru Yoga, is taught as a vital and essential practice. As the guru is a living, breathing human being, he or she is able to deal directly with your ego. Reading a book about how to eliminate ego maybe interesting, but you will never be in awe of that book, and anyway, books are entirely open to your own interpretation. A book cannot talk or react to you, whereas the guru can and will stir up your ego so that eventually it will be eliminated altogether. Whether this is achieved wrathfully or gently doesn't matter, but in the end this is what the guru is there to do, and this is why guru devotion is so important.

Guru Yoga: According to the Preliminary Practice of Longchen Nyingthig

I know of no other book that encapsulates in just 86 pages the essence of Tibetan Buddhism like Guru Yoga does. The author, Dilgo Khyentse Rinpoche, had me from his very first words. This extraordinary adept and teacher of Tibetan Masters is unfortuantely no longer with us in the form you see above. He made the transition in 1991. But he left a record of this teaching for all in an unfolding elegant style that pulls the reader in. Even the intricacies of Tibetan meditation for advanced students are made accessible. While the beginner may want to read another book by the Rinpoche, The Wish-Fulfilling Jewel as an introduction, this one can stand alone. Its contents and practice forms the cornerstone of Tibetan Buddhism.

Guru Yoga is quite simply a vehicle to tie one's heart and path to Guru Rinpoche -- Padmasambhava. Dilgo Khysentse Rinpoche explains the importance of the guru in one's life both physical and etheric. The bond to Guru Rinpoche starts with his mantra:

OM AH HUM VAJRA GURU PADMA SIDDHI HUM

The importance of each word is explained. More importantly the matrix for complex visualizations are given that compliment the mantra. The tapestry he sets for your mind exceeds the grandest of thangkas. The nature of empowerments, an important part of Tibetan Buddhism, is given its proper due. And perhaps the most important aspect we all need in our daily lives—devotion—is treated with a deft touch. How would you like to practice a sense of devotion such as this:

The Essence of Guru Yoga

According to Dilgo Khyentse Rinpoche's book Guru Yoga, "When thoughts arise, we imagine ourselves once more as Vajrayogini, with Guru Rinpoche above our head. There is no need to do an elaborate visualization of the retinue and all the other details. Simply maintaining the presence of the guru above our head, we carry a strong feeling of devotion throughout all our daily activities.

The essence of Guru Yoga is simply to remember the guru at all times: when you are happy, think of the guru; when you are sad, think of the guru; when you meet favorable circumstances, be grateful to the guru; and when you meet obstacles, prayto the guru, and rely on him alone. When you are sitting, think of the guru above your head. When you are walking, imagine that he is above your right shoulder, as if you were circumambulating him. When you are eating food, visualize the guru at your throat center and offer him the first portion. Whenever you wear new clothes, first offer them to the guru, and then wear them as if he had given them back to you.

At night, when you are about to fall asleep, visualize Guru Rinpoche in your heart center, the size of the first joint of your thumb, sitting on a four-petalled red lotus. He is emanating countless rays of light, which fill your whole environment, melting the room and the entire universe into light, and then returning to absorb into your heart. Then the guru himself dissolves into light. This is the state in which you should fall asleep, retaining the experience of luminosity. If you do not fall asleep, you can repeat the visualization again.

When you wake up in the morning, imagine that the guru emerges from your heart and rises up to sit again in the sky above your head, smiling compassionately, amidst a mass of rainbow light.

This is how we can remember the guru and apply devotion during every activity. And should death come suddenly, the best practice then is to blend our mind with the mind of the guru. Of all the sufferings of the three intermediate states, the most intense is the suffering of the moment of death. For this moment there are practices of Phowa, or the transference of consciousness to the buddha fields. The practice of Guru Yoga is the most profound and essential way of doing Phowa.
Finally, this practice of Guru Yoga is sealed with a profound prayer:

> May I and all sentient beings reach the ultimate goal of the path: the
> realization of the absolute nature!
> Having obtained this human body, met the teacher, received
> his instructions, and put them into practice,
> May we make the seeds of the four empowerments blossom into the four
> kayas, so dispelling the four veils!
> By accomplishing the four kayas, may we achieve ultimate
> enlightenment!..." pp. 71, 72

The book ends with "The Guru Yoga Practice, from the Preliminary Practice of Longchen Nyingtik." It's about ten pages of recitations in English and some mantras that definately delivers a radiation and invites the presence of the Master— Padmasambhava.

Guruji Amritananda Natha Saraswati Quotes

Guruji said, "Make information available. Let people take it or leave it, think it is true or false. All that matters is: Are you convinced that this is the way? Let people judge you as they think fit. Tell them 'Come here if you like. Don't come if you don't like. Only try to see for yourself. Don't blindly accept what others say.'"

And also, "I think 95% of learning can be done from your home by yourself with the help of videos and document files. You can post your questions answered also by internet. You are going to need help really in the last mile from a living guru. The highest transmission happens in total silence."

Your body is the real temple in which Mother Goddess lives as life; Every part of your body made by the Goddess holds hidden powers that can be brought out through rituals and meditations involving effort and relaxation; Thereby Goddess helps you to gain knowledge of, gather implements, and manifest the future of your dreams pretty much as you like, rewriting destiny if necessary.

If you make these ideas a part of your mindset, then the magic starts happening. The real Devipuram is your body, and Devi manifests from there.

God and religion is not to be studied or excessively talked about - rather experienced and realized. Religion is unique for all - don't conform to one's views, rather make your own and realize the power of the almighty on a path that you feel is right. God is energy, God is life, God is Love, God is happiness. See *Guruji, page 16*

Merkaba Energy Power Ball of Light & Holographic Sound Healing

"With practice, this ball of energy will become your magical ally providing you with guidance and power."
- Lama Tantrapa

Ricardo's NOTE: Sensitizing the hands with an energy ball in between will enable the Qigong practitioner to attain mastery of being in the flow which can be used as a preparatory practice before doing other meditation and Qigong practices, and also before healing self and others, self-defense and guidance.

- Face east and invoke for divine blessings:
  To the Universal Supreme Being,
  To Buddha Sakyamuni,
  To Buddha Kuan Yin (Buddha Avalokiteshvara),
  To Boddhisattva Mei Ling (Boddhisattva Padmasambhava),
  To all the Great Buddhas and Boddhisattvas,
  To all the Spiritual Teachers, Spiritual Helpers and Hathors,
  Thank you for the blessings of compassionate,
  purifying light and soothing healing energy.
  Thank you for the divine guidance, help and protection

- While standing or sitting naturally, your arms on the side, keep the head upright, slighty tuck in the chin. The top of the head is aligned with the spine; the shoulders are wide. Connect your tongue to your palate and keep the tongue in that position throughout the practice. Gently close eyes and smile from within. Firmly place both feet flat on the ground about hip distance apart.

- Center your body, emotion, mind and spirit by visualizing the central channel (Chong Mai or Tai Qi Pole) as a pranic tube extending from the Bai Hui point on the crown of your head, down the spine, all the way to the Hui Yin point on your perineum (the pressure point between your genitals and anus). Begin to visualize the Qi moving from the Hui Yin to the Bai Hui. Continue to visualize the Qi gliding up and down the pranic tube. Allow the Qi to move up as you inhale and down as you exhale. Continue your gliding of the Qi with slow breathing up and down the pranic tube for 3 minutes followed with Lower Dantien (Hara) Breathing Exercise until you feel calm, relaxed, grounded and centered. Practice Microcosmic Orbit meditation. Read *Return to Oneness with Tao*.

- Press the crown of your head (Baihui) with your forefinger. This is to facilitate concentration on the energy point (crown chakra) to receive heaven Qi (tian Qi).

- Press the soles of your feet (Yongquan) with your thumbs. This is to facilitate concentration on the energy point on the soles of the feet to receive earth Qi (di Qi).

- Press the center of your palms (Laogong) with your thumbs. This is to facilitate concentration on the center of the palms.

- Do the Maitreya (Shiva) Shen Gong and Activate your Omkabah Lightbody with unity mudra.

- Put your hands about 6 inches to 1 foot apart parallel to each other with the armpits slightly open. Visualize a merkaba energy power ball between the hands
  Be aware of the crown of your head, soles of your feet, centers of your palms, the tips of the fingers and the merkaba energy power ball. Inhale and exhale slowly chanting silently "OM MANI PADME HUM." Move your hands slightly back and forth. The movement has to be done very slowly. Do this for about 5 minutes. By being aware of the 5 energy gateways - the crown of your head, soles of your feet, centers of the palms and the tips of the fingers - the head, feet, hand and finger chakras are activated, thereby sensitizing the hands or enabling the hands to feel the subtle energy ball. By being aware of the energy ball between the hands and chanting OM MANI PADME HUM, the merkaba energy power ball is vitalized with energy from the hands, crown of the head, soles of the feet and the mantra. You can also chant the Vajra Guru mantra OM AH HUM VAJRA GURU PADMA SIDDHI HUM.

Eighty to ninety percent of you will be able to feel a tingling sensation, heat, pressure, or rhythmic pulsation between the palms on the first try. It is important to feel the pressure or the rhythmic pulsation.

- Proceed immediately to projecting the merkaba energy power ball to parts of the body, chakras and senses (eyes, ears, mouth, crown of head, forehead, brow, throat, heart, solar plexus, navel, sex, basic) that needs healing and guidance after sensitizing your hands.

  Practice sensitizing your hands and energizing the merkaba energy power ball for about a month. In general, your hands should be more or less permanently sensitized after a month of practice. Do not be discouraged if you do not feel anything on the first try. Continue your practice; it is likely that you will be able to feel these subtle sensations on the fourth session. It is very important to keep an open mind and concentrate properly. Read *Return to Oneness via Pan Gu Shen Gong* to energize the Qi ball with the Sun and Moon energy and expand Qi field.

  Holographic Sound Healing together with the Holographic Light Body Activation as shown and presented here will completely and exponentially amplify the vibration of sound and light body for healing, balancing, body rejuvenation, interdimensional travel, manifestation, ascension and much, much more as I have experienced it in my regular practice and clinical healing application. The *unity hand mudra* is applied during sound healing lightbody activation.

- Chant Sri Vidya mantras Aeem Hreem Shreem (3x) and Aeem Kleem Sauh (3x) with Hamsa to awaken kundalini. The Sri Vidya mantras are best practiced with hand mudras. Read *Return to Oneness with Shiva* and *Oneness with Shiva* to learn more about *Kundalini awakening*.

Why the health care system is broken

Almost all drugs are toxic and are designed only to treat symptoms and not to cure anyone.

- Dr. Alan Greenberg, MD

Overprescribed and adverse side-effects

Doctors are rewarded for prescribing drugs. Big pharmaceutical companies are known to hand out "consulting agreements" worth more than your annual salary to doctors who prescribe their drugs like candy. This is one of the worst practices I can think of that drives a stake right through the heart of healthcare's credibility.

And unfortunately it seems people accept it and take pills for everything.

Have a headache? Take a pill. A rash? Take a pill. Sore muscle? Take a pill. Tired? Take a pill. Overwhelmed? Take a pill. The list goes on and on.

Why do people these days feel the need to take a pill for every ache and pain they have?
What do they think people did before these medications were around?
Why are doctors so easy to prescribe a pill for everything? Is it an easy way out?
Are they getting paid from the drug companies to prescribe them?

"Why don't doctors talk about preventing disease." - Dr Carolyn Dean

Overprescribing of drugs by medical doctors is what makes a health care system broken. No wonder there is a heart attack and opioid epidemic, Alzheimer's and mental health crisis caused by overprescription of statin drugs, painkillers and antidepressants by medical doctors.

"You need to understand that they want you sick and dying, expensively."

- Dr Carolyn Dean, MD, ND

There are natural medicine alternatives to prescription drugs for your general health problems without side-effects such as acupuncture, herbs, acupressure, Qigong, diet, exercise and intranasal light therapy.

The healing process is completely natural in harnessing the power of the body to repair itself. Natural medicine does no harm, respects the natural power of the body to heal, addresses the causes of illness rather than the symptoms (at the mitochondrial level), encourages self-responsibility for health, considers the fundamental health factors, and definitely promotes prevention of diseases. - Ricardo B Serrano, R.Ac.

70-80% of people are magnesium deficient. Magnesium deficiency is a public health crisis of epic proportions. Mitochondria are the powerhouses of cells, producing energy in the Krebs cycle. - Dr. Carolyn Dean, MD, ND

Coenzyme Q10 and Magnesium are essential nutrients required by mitochondria to generate ATP (adenosine triphosphate), and best integrated with intranasal light therapy for healing chronic diseases such as depression, fatigue, diabetes, hypertension, migraine, PMS, insomnia, arthritis, stroke, osteoporosis, asthma, dementia and cancer.

Mitochondrial dysfunction is the root cause of chronic diseases. For more information on intranasal light therapy, read Return to Oneness with the Tao, and The Cure and Cause of Cancer.

Ricardo B Serrano, R.Ac.

Ricardo B. Serrano, R.Ac., a registered acupuncturist, author of Meditation and Qigong Mastery book with Omkabah Heart Lightbody Activation, Serpent of Light Omkabah, and Maitreya (Shiva) Shen Gong Procedure videos, Qi-healer and certified Qigong teacher/ founder of Maitreya (Shiva) Shen Gong and integrative Enlightenment Qigong. He has been trained by Pan Gu Shengong Master Ou Wen Wei, Wuji Qigong Master Michael Winn, Sheng Zhen Qigong Master Li Jun Feng, Master Pranic Healer Choa Kok Sui, Zhan Zhuang Qigong Master Richard Mooney, Merkaba Meditation teacher Alton Kamadon, Sri Vidya teacher Raja Choudhury, Wing Chun Sifu Samuel Kwok and other teachers who are meditation, Qigong, herbal and acupuncture masters.

He has been practicing Wing Chun Kuen, herbology, Qi-healing (Qigong with acupuncture) for over 30 years. He specializes in stress and pain management, and alcohol and drug rehabilitation through natural healing alternative modalities such as counselling, Wing Chun, meditation, nutrition, exercise, Qigong, Qi-healing, intranasal light therapy, acupuncture, herbology, acupressure.

He continues to educate his clients and everyone worldwide through his meditation and Qigong workshops, and holistic websites at holisticwebs.com, qiwithoutborders.org, qigonghealer.com, freedomhealthrecovery.com, qigongmastery.ca, innerway.ca, keystohealing.ca, acutcmdetox.com, quantumnaturalhealth.com, enlightenmentqigong.com and shaktipatmeditation.com. His books are: Return to Oneness with the Tao, Return to Oneness with Spirit through Pan Gu Shen Gong, Keys to Healing and Self-Mastery, Return to Oneness with Shiva, Oneness with Shiva and The Cure & Cause of Cancer.

www.ingramcontent.com/pod-product-compliance
Lightning Source LLC
Chambersburg PA
CBHW081236170426
43198CB00017B/2773